WHO THIS BOOK IS FOR

For anyone who has ever felt loneliness, boredom, dissatisfaction, confusion, heartbreak or existential dread.

For anyone who felt like life was falling apart around them or inside them and wondered how to make things better.

For anyone curious to learn a simple, pragmatic daily application of the principles that inform yoga.

For anyone fed up with seminars, training courses and retreats that give short-lived effects.

For anyone creative, living their art with all the questioning and struggle that process entails.

For anyone seeking a deeper understanding of their own processes.

For anyone seeking richer, clearer connections with others.

For anyone wanting a clear route to sustainable, positive change.

For anyone fed up of drama, fakery and struggle.

For any artistic types with fractious, intense relationships who thrive off the energy contrast but equally become exhausted by it.

For anyone willing to consistently and continuously follow the path to freedom with dedication and trust.

For anyone who wants to live fully.

This is for you.

'It is *not* a question of *learning much*. On the contrary. It is a question of UNLEARNING much.' ~ Osho

CONTENTS

Acknowledgments   5

Introduction   7

Chapter 1 – Remedy – Managing Our Mayhem   15

Chapter 2 – Being Human   18

       Self, the foundations   19

       Know thyself   20

       Real Yoga   23

       Spiritual Bypassing   24

       Stop Taking Things Personally   28

       Self-Enquiry   29

       Early Conditioning   30

       Who am I?   33

Chapter 3 – Reducing Suffering Through Yoga   35

       The Ethics of Yoga – The Yamas   36

       Non-Violence – Ahimsa   37

       Truth – Satya   38

       Non-Stealing – Asteya   40

       Containment – Brahmacharya   41

       Non-Clinging – Aparigraha   44

       The Restraints of Yoga – The Niyamas   47

       Purity – Saucha   47

       Contentment – Santosha   48

       Refinement and Self-Discipline – Tapas   50

       Study of the Self – Svadhyaya   51

       Surrender to The Great Big Everything – Isvara Pranidhana

Chapter 4 – The Limbs of Yoga explained   55

       Move the body – Asana   56

       Breathe well – Pranayama   57

       Withdraw the senses – Pratyahara 59

Focus – Dharana   60
Meditative Awareness – Dhyana   62
Union with the Great Big Everything – Samadhi   64

Chapter 5– Attachment Theory   65
Chapter 6 – Integration & Communication   75

Chapter 7 – Inner Peace   80
Bibliography   82

ACKNOWLEDGEMENTS

I hold enormous appreciation for those surrounding me who have been the catalyst for my moments of epiphany, whether by mirroring or resisting my being – the resulting transformations in consciousness continue to move me deeply.

Thank you to all my teachers so far, especially Charlie, Frank, Simona, David, Wiggy, Stephen, Meghan, Tom, my children – all the people strong enough to be themselves without artifice, who in their perfect imperfection showed me the pieces of myself I had yet to claim that so wanted to be expressed.

Thank you to my children for staying strong in spirit and sweet in nature when things felt difficult, for your patience and mildness as I work relentlessly on my projects, untangle my neuroses and find my way without a plan – Evie and Isaac, I am so proud of who you both are and love you more than I can explain.

Thank you to Tom who has given me children, years of encouragement, friendship and love. Thank you to my sister for the lengthy middle of the night phone conversations that provide a handrail for the stairs up and out of my own drama. Thank you to Emily, Kate, Becky, Tiffany, Kamala, Charlotta and too many other wise, strong women to mention - for your beautiful, uplifting presence. Thank you to my parents for getting me here, onto this planet – the ultimate gift. Thank you to Stephen for educating me, challenging me, teaching me about love without conditions and for being the place from where I realize my strength over and over again.

After everything, there is only ever love left.

*"Understanding without practice is better than
practice without understanding.
Practice with understanding is better than
understanding without practice.*
**And resting in your authentic nature is better
than any understanding and any practice."**
(Upanishads)

INTRODUCTION

freedom and connection

We are made of both magic and ordinariness; our magic inner being whose substance poets, philosophers, doctors and psychiatrists can still not fully explain, and our ordinary human packaging – our bodies and brains.

Learning to access and move from the magic inside that bonds us all yet makes each one of us unique, using only the ordinary and fallible human vehicle we have been given, is both a privilege and a quest.

With deep self-enquiry and strong practice, we can experience the freedom to be ourselves and connect intimately with people, in ways that promote wellbeing and satisfaction for everyone. To experience pleasure, enjoyment and expansion is our birthright and will always 'leave the world a bit better' - as Emerson put it.

The sensations of ease experienced when realizing the freedom to be your true self around others, without artifice or permission-seeking is essential for connection.

We may think we are already free, yet we are run by our minds, our fears, anxieties, conditioning and longings which all affect the body and the ease with which the unique essence of our spirits can be expressed. Burdened by our conditioning and without a structure for harmony it is easy to see faults in others, be overcome with fears and unconsciously find ways of preventing the sense of belonging we desire and naturally seek.

So, though it has taken me a long time to realize it, the evidence I have collected for myself so far, supports the notion that it takes a certain amount of self-discipline to be truly free, to be able to be firmly in command of one's responses and have the ability to source secure footing and true connection whatever the external circumstance delivers.

The reason why so many look for Gods and Gurus to follow is because it is far simpler to do as one is told than it is to go delving inside alone and trust the answers that are found there.

I spent a good portion of my early life bound by rules and regulations and in the subsequent rebellion, spent the next large part of my life with no rules whatsoever. Neither scenario was conducive to sustainable happiness and satisfying relating. I was adept at following imposed structure that was not congruent with my inner being, so I became quite masterful at compartmentalizing myself. Spending so much energy holding parts of self in check vastly reduced my consistence (and confidence) in communication and expression while increasing an already significant tendency to over-analyze, ruminate and get stuck in endless thought loops. My ability to feel connected within – although very fierce and strong – was sporadic and halting rather than a free-flowing natural state. An inherited disconnect between mind and body developed into self-consciousness, passive-aggressiveness and bouts of total abandon where all rules would be flouted, and zero care would be taken for my own wellbeing.

Skipping forward into the rebellion phase, I had no rules, no boundaries, no sense of equilibrium and would flail around in reactivity or push against external structure in an exhausting, haphazard manner. It was as if the real me that I knew was underneath was constantly being sabotaged and prevented from authentic connection, within and without.

Yoga practice finally began reuniting my body and mind (over 20 years ago) and has become a fascinating metaphor for life. Information and wisdom arose from my body like old love letters, unarticulated understandings seeped back into my consciousness, I started to feel, say and be my true self, more often, more eloquently. My spirit started to shine out again. From this innocence - this attunement with self - comes a striking ability to feel what truth really is. My own and other people's. What lies underneath behaviors and words becomes clearer as I see myself in others and them in me. Empathy opens the gateway to intuition and connection that is so often locked with logic. We are each undeniably connected. Deep attention to all aspects of self results in greater awareness of our interconnectedness. The union of yoga ripples outwards.

My communication skills and expression are still catching up with my inner knowing (and maybe always will be) and I consider them a very precious work in progress. The deep resonance I experience with others draws me onwards toward deeper connection with myself through practice which is second nature to me now. I cannot imagine my life without it. The ability to relate well with others, to repair broken connections and to stay present with myself when things feel horribly wrong is what yoga practice gives me.

This book on conscious relating originates from my own experiential process and integrates somatic understanding, reference to the psychology of attachment and a

spiritual perspective based primarily around the eight limbs of yoga. Harmonizing mind, body and spirit results in the deepest of healings - and we all are in the process of healing at some level as we all also have issues with relating. You need only look at your own family to see it.

Understanding of self and the harmony between mind, body and inner spirit are the biggest influencers in relationships and the reverse is also true; relationships illuminate aspects of self that were previously invisible to us. The quality of the relationships we experience depends very much on the relationship we have with ourselves.

We cannot know someone else's experience, this point must be emphasized before we begin as it is the source of so many conflicts – the idea that we know for certain someone else's motives, thoughts or desires is misleading. Until we are practiced enough to see clearly our own limitations and foibles, we will always to some extent project these onto others. Yes, intuition arises in moments of clarity when we are tuned in though remaining fully present enough mid-conflict to utilize it is another thing altogether.

Our behaviors come from our inner experience but are not an accurate representation of our emotions or thoughts, merely signals of them in the same way that a map is not actually the place it represents – it will not help us see what that place actually looks or feels like even though it may give us an idea of the terrain or size.

If we want to communicate on a foundational level with another human being - to enjoy good communication by speaking to this innermost part of them - we would always do well to approach this aim from an investigative perspective first rather than assume our own rightness. We don't know what we don't know.

When we respond to behavior we are responding to the surface signals from that person, not necessarily the truth of who they are underneath. At any point when two people are communicating each have an outer and inner story and multiple filters and interpretations of meaning that are rooted in past conditioning. How clearly someone knows themselves and is able to be congruent externally is a huge factor in how much interpretation is required to truly understand the subtext of their words or actions.

When we use patience and discernment to go beyond the outer level, we have a much stronger chance of not only being heard and understood but of truly understanding the other and most importantly letting them know they have been understood – for in this exchange lies a whole lot of smoothing power in the most difficult of interactions. For real communication to happen we must learn to accurately interpret each other's ways of exhibiting the internal landscape at the same time as leaving mindful space to manage reactions – both theirs and ours. This can only be done consistently and well when we are fully familiar with our own process on an ongoing basis. The more responsibility we decide to take for our communication, the better we become at it.

The alternative is to project our own unresolvedness all over those we interact with and presume meaning that has little to do with them and everything to do with us.

Although it requires some effort, depth of connection is what everyone wants, even and maybe especially those who are reticent to engage at this level (usually due to past traumas).

The state of secure attachment (explained later) this bond engenders creates a startling clarity that can prevent much pain and assist in overcoming many hurdles.

It is a profoundly nurturing space to be in.

It is a metaphorical return to the pre-birth state where all our needs were wordlessly met and we felt only comfortingly held.

Phenomenal growth is possible when we benefit from wholesome connection.

Conscious relating is on another level – one that requires the biggest commitment to self-awareness and growth.

The application of yoga to relating brings the separate psychological, physical, energetic and spiritual aspects, all gracefully together – as you might expect because the word yoga derives from a verb meaning 'to yoke'.

The reams of poetry and prose that have been written about the experience of experiencing another and of experiencing them experiencing us indicates the richness and complexity of relating and how deeply we are affected by it. We are each special combinations of emotion, memory, energy, thought and feeling that logic alone has limited influence over. To understand connection, we must be aware of it somatically, emotionally and energetically, not only with our minds.

Man is a social creature and though our relationships are a necessary part of procreating and flourishing in a physical sense, they additionally have a foundational capacity for repairing of events that have come before us and those that will come afterwards. We do not mend in isolation (though we try) just as we do not get damaged or traumatized in isolation either. In order to fully make the most of this possibility for positive adaptation and healing, it is required that we do the deep work on ourselves that provides grounding and context so that in being fully present to all parts of ourselves we may hold space and compassion for the less easy parts of those we interact with also.

Now (although I still don't like rules much) I prefer to be guided by principles and intention as I find these broader ways of being to have much more power than the limited dichotomous quality of rules that suggest only that one thing is right and another one is wrong. How does this fit into relating with others?

Being in relationship is a descriptor of perspective and relativity. The sun is in relationship to the earth. The sky is in relationship to the ground. I am in relationship to you as another human being. When we hang out together in close proximity, I am in relationship with you as you are with me. All it really means is that we are existing interdependently for a section of time and acknowledging the potential effect we are having on each other. (This is not to be confused with co-dependence – a maladaptive state whereby individuality is lost and both parties are unable to operate independently due to their reliance on the other.)

Biologist Bruce Lipton states that we are all 'one collaborative super-organism' – what you do affects me and vice versa. It is a rare human that survives and thrives alone. And it is almost equally as rare for humans to thrive continuously and harmoniously, in close relationship. without losing valuable aspects of self, energy and creativity.

We are usually surrounded by rules in relationships, most of which are unspoken agreements.

Lovers, friends, business associates, families – whatever structure you find yourself in, there will be a set of rules associated with it that existed long before you entered the picture. The key to harmonious relating lies in making the unconscious conscious, speaking the unspoken, being open about the agreements and expectations that exist in our minds. Knowing ourselves well enough to be able to agree parameters that nurture our growth and happiness and that do not hinder and restrict AND being able to communicate all of this is a tall order indeed. Having a framework and a map is invaluable.

Yoga principles – ancient wisdom of, at the very least, 5000 years ago – lead to cohesiveness and harmony in relating because they are centered around the only thing we truly have control over – ourselves.

The misguided but understandable habit of splitting our experiences (and other people's behaviors) conveniently into good and bad or right and wrong most often leads to awkward, painful encounters and unsatisfactory results.

Misunderstandings, miscommunications, arguments, separations, divorces, ruined friendships, failed businesses and even wars stem from one party adamantly clinging to their rightness. Someone once said: Do you want to be right or do you want to be happy? I used to be hooked on being right and making sure everyone knew it. It was all I knew.

Because the only kind of rightness we can ever own is our own congruence - what feels right for us - when we don't confidently inhabit this or we over-zealously cling to it, it can often feel like the other person is the problem. Setting useful boundaries and taking responsibility for our communication takes practice and patience. It is easier to project out what is right for another based on our values or to make another wrong than it is to pause and ascertain the root of the differences. This causes trouble...trouble that sounds a lot like – "You should have..." or "You shouldn't have..." done, said or felt a certain thing. You can see how quickly this escalates.

As Byron Katie says, there's absolutely no point arguing with reality as you will always lose. So, whether you imagine someone should have or shouldn't have – it is immaterial after the fact because a) they either did or they didn't and b) you are not in control of anyone else or their experience – are you? (Watch out for that one...)

However, the impact someone's behavior had on you <u>can</u> be expressed and that is a different matter altogether, as is expressing it in a way that can be heard without the other feeling blamed, shamed or attacked. I'm not going to pretend this is easy, I mean, if it were, there'd be no need for this book. We will delve into how this can be done like a pro, later.

But I'm jumping ahead. The reason we get so violently triggered by the behavior of others has a lot to do with the parts of ourselves we are not so intimately acquainted with or the shadow as it is commonly known. When you know yourself honestly and well, you know that you have propensity for some not so delightful behaviors. When this is acknowledged, these behaviors, that may be toxic and most likely formed as part of your defense system in early life, can be accepted and adapted if needs be. When accepted in the self – guess what happens next? It is then easier to accept in another. Jason Silva – film maker and futurist – says 'relationships are death practice'. When we use yoga principles to get super clear and honest about ourselves and each other, many ideas, concepts, fantasies and projections start to fall away, and this can feel like violence in the beginning, like a death of sorts. But the ensuing clarity is the path to freedom, to relief from expectations, to a simplicity never before felt, when mind, body and inner spirit are aligned, to a place where we acknowledge that we are the all-powerful creators of our reality and that it's no-one else's job to make us happy? Can you hear that?

How we behave and what we make ourselves available for, no longer must be examined, questioned or argued about in every interaction – we move more often from an inner knowing, a place of internal balance and confidence. This does not preclude mistakes or promise perfection but rather affords us, the wisdom to know what is worth attending to and repairing and, the grace to let what is out of alignment with our true nature, be allowed to play out elsewhere and away from us when necessary

The practice of yoga in its entirety could be described as a manual for managing your energy. You are a package of energy. Thoughts are energy, physical movements are, words are – when we know how to balance and channel our energy and more importantly how not to squander it on making ourselves (and others) miserable – things DO get easier and smoother.

Once you've started to experience the outcomes you prefer and you've sussed how to spend less energy on relating by letting things happen rather than forcing, you'll naturally get more proficient in recognizing your own processes at the same time and life will begin to feel more expansive as you inhabit a state of flow much more often. This flow state cannot help but actualize creativity. Learning how to communicate in ways that other people can hear you and learning how to explain what YOU need to truly hear, see, feel and comprehend someone else – this can make the difference between two well-meaning people entirely missing the mark and a genuine meeting of minds and hearts that results in beautiful connection.

I think it was Edison who said (when blowing up his workshop for the umpteenth time) that he hadn't failed to create what we now know as the lightbulb but had merely found almost 1000 ways of NOT creating it. Many relinquish making themselves available for intimacy in close relationships after the trauma of previous painful encounters – fear closes them down - though cannot give up relationships altogether because of the intrinsic human need for connection we all have. This one-sided connection style results in transmission of pain onto others in a vicious cycle of fear, lack and dissatisfaction.

It is broadly accepted by most entrepreneurs that being unafraid to 'fail' is part of a required skillset if you want to be successful. It is as true in relating as it is in business, albeit more sensitive. And if you wanted valuable insight on the tenacity, flexibility and adroitness required to succeed in the potentially fraught waters of close relationships, someone who has experienced both the thriving, the dissolution and the repair of such (your author) might be a good bet. And this book is as much about repairing as it is creating and maintaining your relationship with self and others. We are always changing while we are alive and as intimidating as that thought may be, it is also full of hope – every breath a chance to start again.

I hold the ancient teachings of yoga in the highest regard, I have solid appreciation for all the teachers who have passed down this wisdom over the last 5000 years or so and it is with honor to this lineage that I present (especially to non-yoga students) a roadmap for their application to human relating in the 21st century.

It is never a good idea to encourage dogma and adhering to the letter of the law mostly leads to ignoring the spirit of it. As the Buddha declared "Believe nothing, no matter where you read it or who said it. No matter if I have said it, unless it agrees with your own reason and your own common sense". My overriding sense has always been one of curiosity. There is an utter relief in having questions answered in the indisputably grounded qualities of the here and now experience – especially somatically. The older I become the more I realize that the body does not lie. The more closely we listen to the body's wisdom, the more easily we can trace and translate the inextricable links between it and the mind and spirit. Getting clarity allows us to have a faith in ourselves that cannot easily be shaken.

Sustainable and impactful change comes from all angles – to be truly integrated it must. I offer you my perspective on these ancient teachings   my deepest and rawest spiritual, physical, mental and emotional experiences – collated as a gift for you, in the hope that you may connect in all ways gracefully and with love and that the world may be a bit better from the sharing of my truth.

Take what serves you from this writing, let it inspire you and leave what doesn't resonate now, until later.

Timing is everything.

All things in balance.

CHAPTER 1: REMEDY

Managing Our Mayhem

The deeply ingrained and universal desire to survive, thrive and feel good with others, drives us to seek connection. It is the most basic human need after survival – to feel that we are not alone.

The past 25 years has seen unimaginable advances in global communication technologies. We have invented innumerable and ingenious ways of reaching each other, however physically far away. Being online and available without interruption has become unquestionably usual. Private, intimate moments of solitude or reflection become scarcer as exposure of self across multiple channels increases and our access to others gets easier and faster. The human urge for connection and kinship remains undeniable and the means to achieve it proliferate - seemingly endlessly.

While we continue to browse and search the virtual world we are constantly bombarded by representations of the global stream of consciousness. The artificial intelligence of our machines ensures automatic and silent manipulation of the data we see, in line with existing preferences and habits, delivering pre-filtered and refined answers that feel comfortingly familiar yet just reassuringly new enough. Our comfort zones are tacitly reinforced. We learn via pre-packaged sound bites and snippets, we use cartoon drawings and symbols instead of sentences to explain our feelings. With every Googled query, another suggestion of content is offered, based on an ever-expanding web of proximal relevance. We are in a loop of our own making. We are being sedated with a self-administered dose of who we must be if we want to be happy and good enough.

Humans are capable of glorious connection, creation and collaboration. At the same time, we are also susceptible to the menacing primal fear of not being clever, beautiful or useful enough to secure our position in the tribe of humanity.

With the rising levels of mind numbing information saturation come comparison-anxiety, fascination-fatigue and plain old disillusionment, leaving us in a garish vacuum where self-realization is delayed and compromised if not fully vanquished. Information being generated and shared at this speed leaves little time for actual learning and self-reflection and while context is eradicated one click at a time, it can feel as though true substance of any kind is rapidly dissolving while an insidious madness seeps into our screen-fried brains.

We may be the most well-informed, privileged generation so far, but we are still in many ways, struggling to connect in ways that feel real and augment confidence and healthy belonging.

From rising diagnoses of behavioral disorders in children to self-harm, anxiety, depression, violence and suicide in teenagers and young men in particular – western society, from the ground up, does not for the most part function as a series of integrated, connected communities.

The high cost of this dysfunction that begins in childhood, is adults who do not have the capacity to go beyond their learned patterns of relating nor have a stable enough internal guidance system to build self-respect, courage and resilience from. When humans are unable to experience healthy attachment, belonging and inner peace the results are chronic emotional and physical problems, broken relationships and unhappiness. Any hope of fulfilling creative potential is lost when all available energy is utilized in steadying fluctuating mental health issues that derive from an intrinsic sensation of lack.

Maybe for this reason – the rise and rise of the self-help industry shows no signs of relenting. It is not as if humans don't need help, a quick glance at geopolitics and the state of the natural world will confirm that we really do. It is that many of the useful aspects of psychology and spirituality have been vandalized by smart-mouthed marketers taking advantage of a deep malaise in the current population to make a quick buck. Much of the well-meaning but misinformed "spiritual" guidance asks us to rise above our human experience without showing us how to understand it, navigate it or enjoy it. Amongst the rehashed, de-contextualized and diluted information on offer, it is hard to locate a solid foundation for growth and evolution of the self.

The prevalence of this confused and fractured rhetoric only escalates the challenge of how best to manage a slew of existing psycho-emotional and physical maladies. In a world of rapidly waning attention spans and huge economic, social and environmental upheaval, how are we to find the sustainable connection both within and without that enables a strong sense of satisfaction, stability and inner peace?

The reconciliation of and the resilience to manage, all elements of our experience is required if we are to experience the natural joy of feeling congruent in body, mind and spirit. When the unconscious patterns and behaviors are made conscious, we are better prepared to be in command of our state. Acceptance of self helps us to see others more clearly and with compassion, thus we start to relinquish the disempowering habit of presuming other people's behaviors are fully responsible for the way we feel.

The state of being human naturally involves painful episodes and the intrinsic instinct to avoid these at all costs.

In the struggle to rationalize an external reality that appears to regularly conflict with our internal feelings, values or instincts, humans have experienced depressions, anxieties, addictions, breakdowns and the physical symptoms and illnesses these states give rise to, since the dawn of time. As Jung stated, 'There is no coming to consciousness without pain.'

Weapons of choice in the fight against inner turmoil include countless variations of manipulating people and circumstance into temporary shapes that agree with our model of how the world ought to be, based on our conditioning so far, or sacrificing our dreams and amputating our natural characteristics to fit the arbitrary perceived demands of the external world.

Both these techniques, whilst in the short term reduce existential agitation, ultimately have injurious consequences for others and ourselves. The unexamined psyche can wreak continuous havoc while left to unconsciously seek its own ends. Side effects include; repeatedly sabotaging the peace, connection, creativity and meaningful action that comprises an enjoyable experience. So, what to do?

CHAPTER 2:
BEING HUMAN

Underneath the noise of today's self-professed experts in personal development and their promises of transformation, is the quiet wisdom of ancient, universal principles in their pure form.

Vedanta is the philosophy of the Vedas, the ancient Indian texts that Yoga derives. Ashtanga mean 'composed of eight limbs' and comes from the Sutras attributed to the ancient Sage Patanjali around 400 BC. The yoga practice that I will refer to throughout this book is also known as Raja yoga or Hatha yoga. Raja – from the Sanskrit – means royal or King and in the beautifully poetic and metaphorical language of Sanskrit, it refers to being regal in the sense of self-mastery, confidence, independence and poise. Raja refers to the goal of yoga rather than the methods employed. Raja yoga is viewed as the state of yoga or unity of mind, body and inner spirit and is focused more on mastery of mind than any physical achievement. Unifying ourselves, becoming one with our true nature and having the self-discipline that leads to freedom is encapsulated by the term Raja yoga. Hatha means sun moon – it is the yoga of creating balance and uniting opposites.

The 8-fold yogic path – an intelligent system of instruction for optimum physical, cognitive, mental and spiritual health - has been utilized for thousands of years. It provides a means to self-knowledge and right action that is of supreme sustainable benefit to ourselves, our relationships, our environment, our communities and consequently the world. It is not a quick fix or a soothing anesthetic, it is a strong medicine with powerful beneficial effects, a self-discipline leading to union and freedom from suffering.

The practical application of these tenets illuminates an understanding of our own existence in time and space and a map of our inner territory that is foundational to handling gracefully (and in some cases transcending) the suffering innate in the human condition. We can only immerse fully into the whole experience of being alive by acknowledging and embracing all aspects of it without separation or avoidance.

To be authentic and successful in relating to ourselves and others, we require robust wisdom and exquisite form to move beyond theory and into living that wisdom. Yoga principles are a solid foundation for self-awareness and right action. A good understanding of how human beings tend to operate provides us with the lubricant to relate artfully rather than as conceited know-it-alls.

We can benefit greatly from the comparatively recent findings on the psychology of attachment theory (as coined by John Bowlby in the late 1960's) which is one of the most important and insightful concepts in understanding the root causes of adult relationship and communication dramas that I have ever come across.

The foundations of nourishing attunement, compassion and adaptation to differing connection styles as described in this framework, gives both relief and hope for each relationship we encounter.

Every aspect written about herein is based in personal experience and discovery, practiced over the years and proven to aid direct and powerful positive change via the nervous system and body.

SELF: THE FOUNDATIONS

"Be regular and orderly in your life...so that you may be violent and original in your work." Flaubert

I approach this subject as someone who considers themselves an artist. To create is an innate human drive – the original drive of life-force. When we are not consumed by the passions that lead to procreating and begetting actual new human life, this force does not simply dissolve.

Our creativity is a signal of life-force, a natural and powerful urge to bring forth beauty, amazement and form. It is no wonder then that we crave scenarios that make us feel more alive by way of awe, bliss and excitement or friction, frustration and contrast. Extremes and imbalance are energetically interesting, causing all manner of physiological changes in the body and psychological triggers in the mind. Mostly, we consciously prefer the high kind of extreme, the exhilaration, the bliss, the metaphorical birth of newness however sometimes we will take any extreme we can get – including destruction - simply to remember the feeling of aliveness surging through us.

With all this life wanting to be expressed somehow through all these different bodies, it's not surprising that it can get chaotic and messy even with the best of intentions. When you consider how many (or how few) have a handle on what is going on internally and a rough idea of how that is translating in terms of outward behaviors, it is clearly amazing that we ever manage to communicate adequately or be harmonious with each other at all.

The perspective of relating is best begun by focusing on ourselves. After all, we are the common denominator in all the relationships we have. If you really believe that everything that goes wrong or hurts you is everyone else's fault, then some of this might be hard to swallow to say the least. I'm not saying it's all your fault either, I'm postulating that a change of angle might just open up some new and positive possibilities that could bring you better results. We all have blind spots, we all like to direct attention toward other people's flaws rather than inspect our own and there is always, always room for improvement while we're still breathing – isn't that beautiful? Every breath a chance to start again.

If we're going to consciously consider ourselves and our behaviors with a view to enabling more happiness, satisfaction and harmony, it's useful to have a framework lest we slide into rumination or self-obsession, neither of which alone is conducive to positive shifts.

KNOW THYSELF

Firstly, I'd like to define what I mean by knowing yourself. I don't concur that the notion of knowing yourself might be a linear task that has a beginning, middle and end. One is enlightened or not, so to speak. No. We are complex beings, we get conditioned in multiple ways from birth onwards – some of it useful, some of it downright damaging – and we are constantly evolving and being shaped by the interactions and events that we encounter. Also, we are human, living in a 3D world – it is not a case of being spiritual OR human. We are both.

Add to this the neuroplasticity of the brain – the ability of our very physiology to morph and change – we are not static objects capable of being defined and understood once and for all. We are packages of consciousness full of moving, changing parts. So really, knowing oneself – the human element - entails knowing a process or having a set of competencies that we can access that allows us to be in awareness (as full and broad as possible) at any given moment. This capability means we can truly comprehend, feel and know how we are interacting with life as we know it at any given moment which gives us massive insights into how we perceive that life is consequently treating us in return. This meta-knowing – how we think about what we think or how we feel about what we feel – is a distinctly human quality, this consciousness sets us apart from other living creatures and fundamentally informs our relationship with meaning itself.

This type of knowing oneself is so much less personal and fraught than the type that declares "this is who I am" or "this is who I am not", this type of knowing has a freedom associated with it that says, maybe more accurately, "I know HOW I am right now, in this moment and thus I know exactly what I desire/require"

This type of clarity, in conjunction with excellent communication that is informed by our higher self is the gold standard of human relating. The path is steep, but the resulting depth of connection is most definitely worthwhile.

Thus, we develop preferences as our practice deepens, some of which change, some stay the same. It is important to know the difference between a preference that we have no intention of changing and one that is open to some degree of flexibility. Defining which parts of ourselves are non-negotiable is a key component in healthy self-worth and easier relating. Conversely, attempting to adapt or soften parts of ourselves that are intrinsic, in order that we get the love or approval of someone else is possibly the quickest route to depression, frustration and self-sabotage available. How to know the difference? We're about to get started on that million-dollar question.

To limit the amount of suffering we undergo from now on and shift perspective on experiences in relating that have caused us pain in the past, we must make the choice to be free.

This conscious choice includes not only deciding what we want but also deciding what we will no longer tolerate or make ourselves available for.

This delineation (commonly phrased as having good boundaries) begins the process of congruently directing our energies towards that which is for the highest good or put another way – it is the decision to focus, intend and move from a strong center rather than be pushed and pulled by the whim of external circumstances. This is the point of a daily mind-body practice.

This practice is not finite, it is fluid. As we develop and gather more intimate knowledge of our character and consciousness, our parameters change or better said - our perception grows to include many truths rather than a short list.

The clarity that ensues when thinking, speaking and acting from our true nature drastically reduces mental noise, indecision and floundering, helping us develop a set of internal mechanisms to guide us towards right outcomes. The definition of right includes morally correct, acceptable, honorable and just, so whether you believe that destiny or fate decide outcomes or that we steer ourselves, both views may be satisfied if we accept that practice refines us into alignment with what is right *for us*. The congruence that ensues from a mind, body and spirit that is both strong and in harmony leads to clarity. When we have clarity, we lessen confusion – for ourselves and those in contact with us.

A lack of self-awareness – or failure to understand our own psychology and blind spots that prevent us acknowledging our psycho-emotional processes (the state of being 'half awake'), contributes to major difficulties in being at home in our own skin. An ill-informed and unsteady relationship with all aspects of ourselves leads unequivocally on to more of the same when it comes to relating with other human beings. Relationships of any sort are always a huge source of debate. The joy and pain inherent in sharing moments with others can be both a fascination and a conundrum where many lose sight of their essence and repeat the same patterns in a seemingly endless and unsatisfying loop. This process runs counter to the progressive and deeply transformative power that relationships have the potential to be, when entered from a conscious vantage point. When one is willing to investigate aspects of self that are called into question via another, there is opportunity for growth, evolution and awakening.

> *"Let me keep my distance, always, from those who think they have the answers. Let me keep company always with those who say "Look!" and laugh in astonishment and bow their heads." Mary Oliver*

Connection is a way in to the existential element of our awareness; the recognition of a bigger presence outside (and inside) of ourselves and our surroundings. However, we describe the unfathomable force that creates worlds, gives our bodies' life force or keeps the planet spinning, the ability to be aware of a greater presence naturally leads to the question of how it manifests in relation to us, how we might interact with it and to what end.

REAL YOGA

How do we become acquainted with our true nature on a regular basis? How do we remain aware of ourselves in a way that encourages connection and growth rather than self-obsession and isolation? The principles of yoga practice deliver truth using our own bodies, minds and experience and when dedicated, this practice is transformative. All the information, resources and power you will ever need are housed in your physical form. Let that sink in. You could not be interacting with life in an emotional, energetic or intellectual way were you not consciousness housed in physical form. The body is transmitting information and clues at every moment, yet we are not generally used to paying the kind of close attention needed to interpret such signals into useful messages. Observing oneself throughout yoga practice (on an ongoing basis) reveals how discipline leads to freedom and freedom subsequently reveals our true nature, shining through all old conditioning and mental projections.

A yoga practice grounded in authenticity exposes the revelatory simplicity of being and from this space, all our connections have opportunity to thrive. Authentic practice will bring up every insecurity, doubt, sorrow and fear that exists within you AND will provide you with the balm to soothe them thus unlocking your potential for joy, pleasure and deep connection.

These spiritual aspects, although deeply felt on an emotional and energetic level, still require gentle polishing if our intention is to live in the world of the ten thousand things and not in a cave on a mountain top.

There are some basic principles relating to human attachment psychology that complement this profound internal process and make acting with integrity from this place, more graceful and less jarring. So, although it is essential to begin our explorations inside, having the tools to translate our insights and wisdom in a way that joins us with others (rather than alienates them from us) is of significant importance when it comes to human relating on any level.

We cannot abandon the human in favor of the spiritual or we would be just as lost as a human with no spiritual awareness. This non-dual understanding is a great contextualizer and though sometimes abused as a means of escaping pain and suffering, it is nonetheless the basis of understanding our true nature. How do we integrate being human with our spiritual aspects?

SPIRITUAL BYPASSING

As we have evolved rapidly beyond the direct hand to mouth experience of survival, we have access to privileges of all kinds, giving us more time for thinking about meaning in general, specifically human behavior (as very few live out their days completely alone) and spirituality.

We are autonomous, but we do not live in isolation.

Human interactions are mutable and complex. Matters of the soul/human spirit cannot be separated from our human condition although they are often misguidedly seen as superior to it. Every aspect of us is an expression of the spirit or life-force within us. Like the weather, some aspects are clement and conducive to harmony and others are violently disruptive to life as we know it. The fact remains that being housed in a 3D body, in this 3D world is the only way we currently have of interpreting the manifestations of the spirit in all its fluctuating glory. All living creatures conform to homeostasis (the avoidance of extremes that would threaten life) of some degree to allow life to continue, which means fluctuations and changes are often met with suspicion if not downright fear. You only need look to the natural world to see that the purpose of life is expansion – to beget life, to evolve, to grow. Balancing the requirement to survive (and thrive) safely, with an unbridled, joyful, creative expression of living fully becomes a constant question to be held up to the light and inspected. It is easy to see how the inclination for safety and comfort and avoidance of pain might lead us towards stagnation and smallness and away from opportunity.

Detailed observation reveals a common trap that prevents expansion and leads to a dulling of feeling and a vastly reduced capacity for connection - the deluded and divisive tendency towards what is now widely known as 'spiritual bypassing'.

First coined by John Welwood in 1984, it involves diluting or dismissing emotional responses to others' or one's own humanity using concepts, philosophies and platitudes to retain a perceived modicum of control and avoid honest self-reflection or responsibility. Rooted, usually, in legitimate intentions for peace and a desire to escape any looming threat to our carefully constructed identity, this phenomenon proclaims that love and light or destiny trump all - without discernment - like a safe, comforting blanket to hide beneath. Either refusing to call out toxic behavior or excusing one's own, without shining awareness on such discomforts as they arise, creates a false veneer of unity within and without, that prevents development and reinforces separateness. How so?

Ignoring the impact and consequence of flawed human behavior does not make it disappear.

All actions result in karma. One might equally say for every action there is an equal and opposite reaction (Newton's third law). Maintaining the illusion of peace while denying any felt experience creates residue in the body and the heart-mind. This residue not only affects the physical body but forms filters in our consciousness through which we view and affect any subsequent experiences, clouding our discernment and adding to the 'samskaras' or grooves that prevent clear awareness.

Hasty declarations of so-called higher wisdom, given before the human processing has run its natural course, are merely a temporary coping mechanism designed to keep us where we feel safe and unchallenged, reducing the capacity for positive change and increasing the probability of incongruent, disconnected relating with ourselves and others.

In the refusal to acknowledge or be with our own pain and discomfort, we limit the ability to see and be present with it in others and consequently we refuse to link the impact of our actions with the effects they have on other people. Not looking at the impact of our choices or behaviors on others may make it far easier to not take responsibility for them though it makes it far harder to enjoy good mutual connection. Unresolved trauma proliferates. To the extent that we reduce our awareness of any aspect of self, we become less adept at remaining in connection. What is denied in self becomes denied in other, replaced with judgement and fear. The desire to be heard, seen and felt and thus connected is great in humans and cannot be substituted, though addiction and violence to subtle and varying degrees will often take its place. The inability to connect gracefully with others means we carry huge potential for unwittingly becoming an instrument of their pain and at the same time remaining willfully blind to this. Counter to the righteous intention for peace, connection and positive influence, we become walking disasters of unintegrated and mismanaged reactions, ready to fire off harmful responses that perpetuate suffering. The intention is a pipe dream prevented from actualizing by our own refusal to see clearly and act according to what is being presented to us.

Spiritual bypassing is a convenient tactic for abnegating all personal responsibility and anaesthetizing pain – a convoluted trick to absolve us from the consequence of our here and now experience of living. (You can see the appeal...) Furthermore, when insisting on willful blindness to our own faults, we usually also dismiss the potential of our own greatness. If love, light and destiny run the show why do we bother to get out of bed in the morning? Because we are here to participate! The dimming of our own light results in dissatisfied frustration, depression and graceless derision of others that do well. We play small to stay safe. Without the integrated heart-mind and body that is based in good awareness and processing and that allows energy to flow freely we are much more likely to get stuck with expression whether that be sexually, emotionally or creatively. It takes courage to do this work both in terms of fully inhabiting your potential and deeply connecting with others.

If the ultimate intention is harmony, enjoyment, thriving and positive action that unites rather than divides, how are we best to make room for all the varying perspectives and levels of competency we will encounter in our close relationships and communities? How do we use universal principles, not as escapism but to support living well and fully NOW?

By living as if we are all one, even when we have no proof or belief that this is so. Soham in Vedic philosophy means I am that or identifying ourselves with what I like to call the Great Big Everything and knowing that it is in everyone and everything. 'I am that' implies that we can be that, we can have been that in the past or may still be that in the future. It implies that there is no separation. It speaks of the divine spirit in each of us and of the perfectly imperfect human manifestation.

It is not another 'spiritual' stick to beat oneself with, the 'everyone is a mirror' misnomer that assumes each and every instance of idiotic or hurtful behavior that comes into your orbit represents a piece of yourself you are blind to. Sure, we can check our personal integrity using this – it can be useful – but its real value lies in the potential of its meaning.

More resonant with 'there but for the grace of God go I' – this tenet encourages temperance in our dealings with others. Our perception of others depends very much on the clarity with which we can observe ourselves. Pausing for clarity (as it is rarely found in the midst of reactivity) before responding not only reduces any negative charge we may add to a dynamic but provides necessary space to look behind the words or behavior and welcome the glimmer of spirit along with the messy, fucked up human it resides in and in doing so – welcome ourselves. All of ourselves. Kindness results and kindness is one of the best environments for humans to flourish in.

There are no absolutes. Our black can easily be someone else's white. Communicating with care and precision becomes an essential foundation to defining and maintaining the kind of personal boundaries that act as a container for our growth not an inhibitor to it. It is a wise and kind action therefore to know oneself, accept oneself and communicate often the parameters that constitute healthy relating. This way, we provide full opportunity to ourselves to receive in alignment with who we are and full transparency for others. Because conscious, awake humans are constantly evolving and choosing - our preferences and boundaries have proclivity for change too. Close, clear awareness on our own processes and current limitations together with authentic communication minimizes the risk of becoming a confusing and potentially damaging force upon others. To the extent that we are willing to assume full responsibility for our communication and how it lands with the other, we are not only stating clearly who we are and how we wish to be met/treated but also giving others the option to choose and adjust correspondingly in line with their values. Our clarity gives them clarity, promoting agency, confidence and a smooth easiness which is far from the blaming, inflammatory, disingenuous space of manipulation and co-dependence that can only flourish in disconnection.

INTERDEPENDENCE – A NATURAL STATE

If we are to remain focused on being a force for good wherever possible, while honoring the realization that life unfolds in ways that we cannot fathom or control, then it is essential to take care of our awareness, to polish it, to look curiously and honestly at the things we would rather gloss over and ignore. To be fully informed about our own tendencies and reactivity to more ably access our equilibrium. This equilibrium is the answer to being present, engaged and feeling secure as we embrace a life of unknown potential. It is the bridge between differences and the balm to mitigate drama and hurt. Acknowledging the social nature of humans and how we affect each other is a key component in even wanting to take this approach to living in the first place.

Until we admit that we need other humans, that we have an effect on each other and that our choices and actions define that effect - we are dangerously arrogant in our perspective. Though we may benefit short term by imagining we can never be at fault (because: destiny) our actions then have no context other than of our own making and without context, they also have very little meaning. When we see the lines of cause and effect between ourselves and other humans, rather than being self-referencing automatons, both accepting and offering support becomes instinctually pleasing and mutually beneficial for growth and expansion.

Staying in clear awareness is a practice. It is only ever a snapshot. You don't do the work, reach wisdom then stop. It is a constant process. Good knowledge of the human self is only ever temporarily realized because we are always changing. Although our true nature is ever-present and ever-the-same, and it is without doubt essential to tap into this as often as possible – the point is – we are spiritual AND we are having a human experience. The human part is messy, chaotic, unruly, changeable and diverse and the point of any spiritual practice is not to change that but to be at peace with it, to do our best to respond with equanimity, to minimize negative impacts on ourselves and others, to create harmony and bring our creative urges to fruition to breathe and exist in the world.

As we expand in line with the nature of the life-force that informs our existence, it is natural to have more compassion not less. More connection. More creativity. More patience and understanding with the difficult path of the human. It is hard to be present with pain and it is just as hard to be present with heart-breaking beauty, but we were not meant to hold onto it. We are the conduits, the channels through which life wants to flow, wants to express its wonder and wants to play with its own creations in the form of us and our fellow humans.

STOP TAKING THINGS PERSONALLY (THE EMPTY BOAT)

The idea that someone else can be responsible for one's reactions is compelling indeed. You made me angry/sad/anxious is a common complaint in any relationship. One of the problems with this habit is that if we are to blame others for the bad feelings we experience then we must also look to them for the good too – at best disempowering and at worst a speedy route to delusion, bitterness and apathy.

In the usual course of human dealings, we encounter other people's realities with either smooth enjoyment or jolting unease. To the extent that we are caught in our own view of who we are and who we are not, how adeptly we can communicate our boundaries and preferences and what story we tell ourselves about how benign or otherwise life is; we will find it challenging to absorb experiences without getting ruffled.

When I say ruffled, I mean, pissed off, saddened, frustrated or any other feeling that is uncomfortable to sit with. Whilst all these emotions are without doubt part of the human experience, we hope to accept them with grace when they occur rather than purposefully seek them out or prolong their occurrence. We're here to enjoy it after all.

One of my favorite parables is this old Zen story accredited to Chuang Tzu:

There was a man who had a boat. He loved his boat very much and would often sail it out on the lake. One misty morning, he took his boat out onto the lake, it was quiet, peaceful and still but the mist was thick, and it was hard to see very far beyond the edges of the boat. He was enjoying the stillness and feeling very relaxed. Suddenly there was a jolt and a thud as another boat collided with his own. The man, shaken and incensed, shouted in anger "What the hell are you doing? Can't you look where you're going?" He stood up, his own boat rocking wildly, making fists of his hands, he became hot with rage. Standing up, barely keeping balance, he stared intensely and crossly through the mist waiting for an answer and receiving none as he drifted, the other boat bumping gently against his own. As the mist cleared a little he saw that the other boat was empty, just an abandoned, old thing that was floating here and there on the water. He sat down, deflated, relaxed his hands, momentarily perplexed and observed the tension beginning to leave his body.

■■■

In the story, no-one purposefully crashed the boat, it was a random happening. When the man imagined that it was a deliberate action meant to disturb his peace or carelessness, of course he was naturally angry. As he realized there was no ill intent towards or personal disregard of him, he relaxed and took notice of how upset he had become.

When we have a run in with someone who upsets our peace, it's easy to get overwhelmed with reactivity before we notice the metaphorically empty boat that caused our upset. Discernment (viveka) is needed to locate which part of our psyche got triggered into freaking out. Mostly, the current problem is not really the problem, only a trigger point that brings up the residue of past instances of being disrespected, wronged or hurt. When we know the difference and practice being aware enough to inspect the details of our own reaction, we naturally enjoy more spacious and calmer relating.

Taking enough care of your own peace to warrant asking self-searching questions and answering them honestly, with patience when you get upset, leads not only to a much clearer understanding of the situation at hand but also familiarizes you with your own tendencies (**samskaras**). And when we know better, we do better.

SELF-ENQUIRY

What criteria do you use to distinguish between environments and behaviors (others) that challenge you and promote growth and ones that damage you? Can you tell the difference?

Are you more likely to retreat or react and speak up when faced with conflict? Could a rebalance of this tendency improve the quality of your connections?

What is your biggest fear when faced with conflict? If this is too broad, then think of the last 3 conflicts you experienced – is there a theme?

Think of a situation that prompted you to make a new personal boundary. How does that boundary serve you? Was it made in reactivity, protection or with good discernment? How would it feel to adjust it now? Would changing it help or harm you?

> "We spend most of our lives assuring each other that our costumes of identity are on straight" Ram Dass

Who do you think you are? How attached are you to your labels? Mother, Father, Wife, Husband, Lover, Business-woman, Artist, Yogi, Risk-taker, Peacemaker, Daughter, Son etc. ad infinitum - and all the qualities that accompany each descriptor – do you realize how subtly and strongly the words we use to describe ourselves affect our behavior and the results we subsequently experience, even if those words are only in our minds? Language requires we learn labels from a very young age – we are shown objects and given the code – block, toy, spoon, mummy, daddy – so we can make ourselves understood. Further on, the labels become more complex in nature. Behaviors are labelled as good or bad, nice or horrid and so on, each one with its own emotional response that manifests in the body. How this begins and develops is integral to our understanding of now and our awareness of how we have organized our minds and our lives. Where we come from and where we think we are currently situated has an impact on where we imagine we can go and what we think we can do. Our early conditioning defines our patterns of attachment and our tendencies, it's good to have a basic overview to give shape to our awareness of self.

> "He that does not know history is doomed to repeat it" ~ Edmund Burke (1729)

EARLY CONDITIONING, A BASIC OUTLINE

Our behavior, as babies, is instinctive and without self-consciousness.

It is designed to activate in others, the required care-giving necessary for our survival because we are unable to care for ourselves yet. We have awareness of discomfort, fear of falling and loud noises along with a multitude of new sensations not formerly experienced within the warm, safe confines of the womb and thus we struggle and cry until bliss or oneness is resumed.

We are perpetually seeking the experience of oneness, of undivided consciousness. Our survival and growth depend on our needs being met, no longer automatically sustained by the umbilical cord and housed in perfect comfort, we need food, warmth and touch, and so it makes sense that the process of intuiting and communicating lack be an efficient one. We make loud, attention-grabbing noise until someone comes to our aid.

When we are old enough (generally sometime before we go to school) to become conscious that we have an effect on the world outside of us and that that world can also impact us – the predicament of the human condition starts in earnest. As we learn more about the external world and start gathering language and names for things, we start describing the story of our experience and getting more familiar with duality.

We mentally describe our experience with reference to our perception of 'otherness' or that which is not us. Infant is separate to mother, mother leaves and returns, pleasant feelings and unpleasant ones.

The information we perceive from around us as we grow helps create our initial logic [black and white] and way of comprehending and informs our particular version of what is good or bad. As we naturally strive to survive and remain protected and one of the pack, we adapt our behaviors, thoughts and assumptions to fall in with what is being shown to be acceptable by the adults close to us; mostly we are rewarded when we tessellate well with both their overt and tacit belief structures and often we are punished when our behavior contradicts them. From toilet training to sleeping and eating patterns, our bodily functions are regulated to varying degrees, dependent on our caregivers. We learn to do what works best for our comfort and safety and what minimizes unpleasant consequences and reactions and thus we construct a story of 'the way things are' that helps us learn more quickly, maintain good relations and reduces instances of conflict. The mind is literally shaped, synapses are created and strengthened. Reality as we know it, is constructed.

To protect the fragile identity of the self (id) and continue to get its needs met in this new reality, the ego develops, thus structuring our reality in dualistic terms for the first time.

We learn what to do and not do and what to say and not say – by extension also – what to think and not think. We learn how best to be in order that we can survive. In so categorizing our experience, we gather a composite understanding of who we are based on the assumed clarity of who we are not or cannot safely be. As time progresses, if this initial logic is left unexamined, the essence of our adult selves can end up bearing little or no resemblance to the child we once were before this unconscious manipulation began.

As our autonomy develops, childish innocence mixed with encroaching awareness of trauma, unkindness, injustice, hatred and other divisive behaviors outside of us, triggers instinctual resistance that augments this dualistic thinking. We strive to remain on the side of good and right to secure the love, affection and safety from outside of ourselves that makes us feel good. By refusing to identify with what is 'bad' or 'wrong' we strengthen our attachment and allegiance to its opposite and thus further guarantee our physical survival even if the mind experiences conflict.

TEENAGERS

The pre-teen and teenage years, long maligned as a period of self-indulgent introspection and acting out, are maybe the first instance of epiphany we experience in relation to the human condition. Leaving the innocence of early childhood, our personality develops, and our capabilities increase, and the primary caregivers naturally retreat. The prospect of independent survival in some form seems viable to us. We begin to question.

The parameters imposed on us (and self-appropriated out of necessity) are no longer essential to guarantee our existence. We become more fully aware of choice and the possibility of rebellion now that we are not solely reliant on our care-givers. There is great friction between the drive to become independent and the compulsion to remain close to the original source of safety and love. The healthy ideal of attaining gradual independence without relinquishing the love and support of parents is often elusive.

This may be the first time we feel truly alone and have the sensation of 'losing' our minds in confusion. Self-harm, suicide, anxiety and depression can surface and be prevalent in these years. At this precipice between child and adult, the desire to form alliances with a collective whose ideals are more congruent with our inner, authentic self, often takes over. The clothes we wear, the music we listen to, the language we adopt – all are signifiers we collect to strengthen our conviction that this fledgling identity/self in its transitioning form, has a home and belongs.

Some cultures still retain the useful tradition of initiation for girls and boys crossing the threshold into adulthood – a challenge undertaken alone that exorcises many existential demons in one fell swoop and honors this transition with ceremony. By proving their skills, autonomy and will to power the child becomes truly independent.

YOUNG ADULTS

At the next stage of development there comes recognition that we are not one dimensional and neither is our experience. Pair-bonding accelerates our awareness that things are neither as simple nor straightforward as we had hoped. We start to decipher the multi-faceted, complexities of human beings and the ambiguities contained in the world around us as we continue to form relationships, have new experiences and refine our character.

What seemed plain becomes elaborate – our awareness of the world and of others, expands. The more consciousness expands, the more problematic it becomes to accept without question the concept of such binary thinking as we have been used to. Being defined by a group or single idea or the premise that things, people or behaviors can be isolated neatly into categories of good or bad seems childish and unrealistic. The notion of this or that gives way, sometimes agonizingly, to this AND that. We are confronted with the reality of 'grey areas' and the possibility of our relatedness, however tenuous to many things, including that which we find loathsome in others. Conscious, awake individuals who want to continue making sense of the world whilst maintaining preservation of the self, must resign themselves to the difficulties innate in answering the question: Who am I?

WHO AM I?

The consciousness that is adequately developed to ask such a question is predisposed to fear of and guilt about the outcome. As part of our biology we have retained a craving of acceptance from the clan lest we be banished and unable to survive.

The tendency to habituate showing the parts of ourselves that are celebrated, loved and applauded and hide the bits that are rejected or misunderstood, is commonplace. In calculating the probability of favorable results, we must also accept the prospect of the alternative. If who we find ourselves to be, deep down, does not tally with the prescription we were given as children or with the confines of the life we now find surrounding us as adults – then what?

What happens if I am bad? What if I am not good enough? What if I am wrong? What if I expose the truth of who I am, and I am rejected, shamed or abandoned?

The avoidance of pain, signaling harm or threat to our existence, is hardwired into us as part of our survival mechanism – we are programmed to survive.

Ever since the first delayed reaction to our signal cry, the first time we were told 'No' or the first feeling of embarrassment or shame – we have accumulated evidence of how we ought to be to ensure our own comfort and survival. While the subconscious memory of submitting to external forces to ensure continued comfort and happiness may be strong and insistent, it is vital that we correlate our present happiness with the quality and direction of our own thoughts, words and actions.

Differentiating between our conditioning (past) and our present – this present moment – is essential to reprogramming the body's old fear responses and the mind's habits, for natural health and expansion and to prevent stasis and regression. Our resting state is one of effortless love and ease, figuring out how to return to this as easily and as often as possible is a worthwhile pursuit indeed.

CHAPTER 3
REDUCING SUFFERING
THROUGH YOGA

To understand the transformative power of yoga it is important to include all its aspects, not reduce it to just the well-known physical limbs of postures (asana) and breathing (pranayama).

Here the 8 limbs are described in practical terms and though yoga is absolutely a personal practice, the effect of a practicing with integrity ripples out beautifully and interminably to everyone in your orbit. For interpersonal relations to make good sense we must first be capable of taking command over our own selves, this is certain.

Taking personal, ethical responsibility for the relating we are involved in quickly brings clarity (for us and others) that guides us through **the potential pitfalls thrown up by our** humanity – emotions, thoughts, habits and conditioning become clearer and less charged through the lens of yoga. It is not that yoga principles exist to reduce the intensity of our experience but rather to see it more clearly as experience, as one version of reality or truth, amongst many, with a wider view in sight. From this steadfast vantage point we are free to respond rather than react and will more easily regain equilibrium after episodes of destabilization.

Understanding the basic limbs of yoga creates a different filter for the mind. Situations and interactions can be viewed through this filter and responded to differently. Happenings that may have previously caused only pain and difficulty can be seen as opportunities for refinement, learning and recalibration, helping us get clearer about who we are and what we intend. When yoga is practiced regularly, it spills over into everyday living until all of life becomes yoga – union with all that is – naturally reducing conflict and suffering.

YAMAS (ETHICS/INTEGRITY)

These are the ethics of yoga.

The yamas outline the principles that underpin yoga.

This is the beginning, the introduction, to a yogic way of being.

For each of the yamas and niyamas, then each of the remaining 6 limbs of yoga, we will look at how they can be applied to self and thus to our ways of relating and connecting.

It is key to remember that these principles apply to mind and body, attention to which will give rise to a fuller, clearer expression of inner spirit and the state of congruence and flow that follows.

This section is designed to be used for self-enquiry. It contains questions that will help you reflect honestly on how aligned you feel to these principles. Answering honestly will give clues as to which areas of your life might be smoothed and improved by a more delicate awareness of self and how this might further impact the relating you are involved in.

Be gentle with yourself by resting in awareness and observance of yourself without judgement.

These principles have a soft strength that will support you through the natural dissolving of old habits that have led to unwanted results and can provide a solid foundation for lasting positive shifts and the preliminary destabilization that sometimes occurs when settling into new ways of being.

Experiment with using them in your daily life and watch the results – it is only then that they will have real meaning.

Take your time on each section, write notes if you like and revisit it each time you feel stuck.

Shining the light of awareness into your own consciousness is the foundation of conscious connection with others.

Truth is a spectrum and as humans, we see different elements of it each time we experience learning. Authentic meaning comes through existential experience.

AHIMSA (NON-VIOLENCE)

Himsa means injury or harm – the 'a' denotes the opposite of this. To do no harm.

Being respectful, mindful and compassionate are all opposites of causing harm. Investigating how we treat ourselves is at least two-fold.

How we look after our bodies and what we focus on or allow space for in our minds are both important aspects of ahimsa.

Our physical form requires nourishment, exercise and affection to thrive. What does practicing ahimsa toward your body entail? Eating healthy, fresh foods full of vital energy means our bodies can function well using the right nutrients to support our systems and without the stress caused by poor digestion. Moving the body to increase blood flow and strengthen the muscles and bones helps us enjoy better sleep, mood and brain function.

Thinking of eating and exercise as acts of love toward ourselves can remind us to practice ahimsa.

Similarly, what we feed our minds on has an effect. Filling the mind with troubling news items, problems and criticisms strengthens our fear responses and propensity for further fault finding and inhibits the mind's ability to allow joy and relaxation.

When we take loving care of our body and mind, the spirit tends to be strong and bright as a result.

When our spirit feels dull, it can be useful to check in with body and mind first and become aware of what we have been ingesting as well as any areas we might be overlooking. Contextualizing our experience is super important if we are to hold a healthy perspective that supports us. The media, the conversations, the energy of our environment and the people we are around, all have a distinct effect on our spirit, most significantly if we are sensitive (or have inadequate boundaries) and tend to absorb rather than observe. (More detail in brahmacharya section) What has been surrounding you or happening in the last 7 days? Often it can be soothing to acknowledge what we have been dealing with and that we are still functioning despite it all. Can you give yourself encouragement instead of criticism?

Sometimes our emotions and energy are impacted by events that are difficult to deal with. At these times it is especially important to ask the following questions:

What activities nourish your spirit? When is the last time that you: Communed with others? Rested? Spent time alone in a pleasant space or in nature? Expressed your creativity? Practiced self-love or pleasure?

Later on, we will discuss accessing and directing the phenomenal power connecting the body and mind. These two parts of the same system are our vehicle for traversing life, the state of them both influences the clarity with which we can perceive the spirit that is housed within and the strength of our ability to express it into the world.

It is often said that the critical voice of our mother or father becomes our own internal voice. Psychologist Edward L. Thorndike (1874–1949) was the first scientist to study operant conditioning – the manipulation of behavior using reinforcement or punishment. Do you remember the words or phrases that were aimed at you when you exhibited an unwanted behavior? Most likely. Even the most well-intentioned parents will still condition their children in ways that are not always useful or positive. As a result, we can judge ourselves harshly and repeat the type of reprimanding or punishing response toward ourselves in later life.

These deterrents that were often misguidedly meted out, can leave us with a warped view of our personality or nature. Maybe we were told off for being loud, funny or 'too clever'? On inspection, we may realize that we have been subconsciously editing ourselves ever since to align with an authority figure whose values were never questioned. Alternatively, we could also be harshly responding to our own human behaviors (criticism, jealousy, anger, sadness or impatience to name a few) rather than lovingly accepting them and deciding to take on the learning so we can do better next time. Either approach can be seen as a violence toward the self.

SATYA (TRUTHFULNESS)

The word sat translates as true essence or true nature.
This yama signifies a lot more than not lying.
Our true nature is perfection.
We are sheathed in human form and live in a 3D world of infinite texture and quality and a great deal of illusion (*maya*). When we are focused on outward appearances, on things that trigger discomfort or sadness or the qualities and behaviors in others that irritate or upset – it is easy to forget the beauty and simplicity of our own true nature and it is harder to see it in others.

Although what feels true for us (preferences/beliefs/thoughts/feelings) changes over time, our true nature does not change, it is constant and certain. However deeply held and strongly attached to, our opinions, when expressed carelessly, cause disconnection but truth, ultimately, does not. *

Practicing satya starts by getting into alignment with our own true nature and then thinking, speaking and acting with integrity towards it.

Using satya to inform the way that we express ourselves, we see that even our most closely held 'truths' such as feelings and thoughts, are subject to change due to the very nature by which they were created, and the changing perspectives brought on by the finitude of life and the passing of time.

Thoughts and feelings are part of the human experience that exist alongside our true nature, helping us interact in the world and experience being human.

Anything that is subject to change cannot by nature be absolute truth.

In this case, when expressing ourselves and delivering what we feel to be true for us in any given moment, it is imperative that we take ownership of these thoughts and feelings if we want to encourage open, peaceful connections. After all, our observations of the present moment are always colored to some extent by past experiences - including fear and pain – that sometimes prevent us from seeing or hearing another clearly.

Taking ownership does not guarantee our rightness or even that our expression will be well received by another, but by practicing satya, we remain in alignment with our integrity and take responsibility for our opinions, recognizing their transience and not casting them as unfair judgements onto other people. In this way we mitigate perpetuating suffering, minimize harm and maximize the chances of remaining in connection.

Marshall Rosenberg, a psychologist and the founder of Non-Violent Communication, explains very clearly that the purpose of this kind of communication is to connect in a way that engenders natural giving. His passion for developing NVC stemmed from his personal experiences of anti-Semitism and (in his own words) it "evolved out of my practice with people who were hurting and experimenting with what might be of value to them, whether they be in the correctional school for girls, or people labeled schizophrenic."

Rosenberg also had a strong grounding in zazen meditation from the Zen Buddhism tradition – the concept of satori is similar to true nature as discussed here and meditation is part of the eight-fold path and of many other Eastern teachings. (Zen Buddhism is a mixture of Taoism and Mahayana Buddhism which both originated around the same time as Yoga)

He goes on to say that playing the game of who is right (or who has truth?) leads only to punishment or reward, if you're right you get rewarded, if you're wrong you get punished. Guilt, shame and violence result when we make ourselves or others wrong and there is no room for multiple realities as seen by different individuals. We are arguing about opinions and getting lost in *maya* (illusion) of this world, adding to suffering. Meditation (discussed later) practice helps us make space between the fluctuations of the mind and the awareness that is our true essence, helping us recognize ourselves and differentiate between profound truth and the noisy details that distract and separate us. When we experience as an observer of our own thoughts, it is easier to imagine the difficulties that others may have in communicating their truth to us and make room for understanding.

Comprehending truth as something that is inherent in each of us (our true nature) helps us to temper our differences and view rightness and wrongness as matters of perspective only.

Everyone has a sense of satya, inner knowing, a gut feeling, an intuition – how are you aware of yours? How do you tune into it? Have you ever overridden it? Is so, what happened?

Whether someone can hear us (or us hear them) or is ready, willing and able to hear us does affect connection. Acting from satya means we communicate from our true nature, a place of kindness, non-judgement and truth that leaves no residue. The place where our highest selves can meet. Accessing this place takes tenacity and a solid practice, even with these you'll still mess up at times. Satya is one of the key elements in repairing broken connections which is detailed in Chapter 6.

ASTEYA (NON-THEFT)

Steya derives from the Sanskrit word for something that can be stolen.

Non-stealing seems simple enough. Deeper understanding of this yama delivers some unexpected areas where we might further hone our behaviors to promote peace and reduce suffering.

How can we apply this to ourselves? How can this apply to our relations with others?

Are you aware of excessively taking from others who will freely give to you? Just because you can, or you've got used to it? Might you be taking advantage of someone's energy because they have poor boundaries? It is easy to say that we are not responsible for the actions of others, of course, but when we become aware of our collusion in their harm, remaining in our integrity guides us toward right action and away from manipulation. Yes, the lines can be hazy but the person with the most self-awareness and aptitude in any given situation, always has the biggest responsibility to act according to the highest good. Non-action can be just as damaging as wrong action...

Consider the following:

Are you punctual? Do you say what you mean? Do you ask for more than is fair when you know the other person has difficulty refusing **you**? Do you say yes to things that you have no intention of doing? Do you allow others to entertain ideas about you that are untrue just because it makes you feel good? When we allow untruth to exist (when we know it to be untrue) without shining the light of awareness onto it, we are potentially taking away this truth from another and thus preventing them from making informed decisions that serve them.

Allowing someone to believe a lie because it serves us is as unethical as telling a lie for our own benefit. It's human and it happens and when we become aware, we avoid it. As Maya Angelou says, when you know better, you do better.

BRAHMACHARYA (CONTINENCE/MINDFULNESS/CONTAINMENT)

This Yama is often misunderstood as just pertaining to celibacy or fidelity in marriage. Its literal meaning is 'going after Brahman' (another name for the Supreme Reality, Self or God) or 'the way of the Divine' - whether you perceive that as God, Goddess, Universe or Other.

The nuanced meaning of this yama, for a practical application, is more akin to 'right use of energy' or mastery or conservation of one's energy.

In the 21st century western world we can have a rather distorted perception of sexual energy as a distinct and separate part of us – a desire that requires satiating or a disruptive force to wrangle with.

Though a fair portion of our awkwardness, ambivalence and misunderstanding of sexual energy stems from a patriarchal system and Church that has wanted to control it, in Eastern traditions, it was broadly understood that sexual energy was THE energy, the prana, the chi, the vital life –force that IS us,

This distinction is important.

Expressions of sexuality are expressions of energy just like thought and emotion. Understanding how we direct our energy is key to the application of this yama.

Viewing sexual energy only as currency or as a means to get physical pleasure and climax is missing the huge potential of this force.

Organized religion is not unaware of the huge power resting in sexuality and set about structuring ways to contain and diminish it many centuries ago. Confining sexual activity to marriage and conflating sexual ecstasy with sin helped replace joy and creativity with fear and shame – two of the most powerful control mechanisms known to humans and an excellent way of making sure their adherents used all available energies in service of the Church.

In more ancient times, dating back to 5th & 6th century BCE, monks and sages practiced brahmacharya by foregoing sexual activity in lieu of service to the Divine. Interestingly though, this was not a requirement for householders and therefore suggests abstinence was based neither in puritanical reasoning or used as a control device but was understood as a prioritizing of vital energy use in line with one's life path or dharma.

Skillful management of one's energy in service of the highest good of everyone can take many forms and following the way of the Divine does not always connote celibacy though does entail acknowledgement of sexual energy as a force and a subsequent mindfulness around the impact we allow it to have on our lives as a whole.

Sexual energy is honored in the yogic traditions as a natural and powerful part of our humanity, not to be repressed but rather to be channeled and acted on in ways that maintain our respect for it in ourselves and others.

There is a sacredness in physical acts of love that can go far beyond satisfaction of human sexual desire and toward a clearer knowledge of our connection with the Divine.

Mindfulness around our sexual activity to avoid harm makes sense when you acknowledge the great power that sexual energy derives from, after all it has to capacity to create new life.

Practicing brahmacharyra may include choosing not to indulge in sexual pleasure when there is a negative payoff to ourselves or another. When practiced in conjunction with the other limbs of yoga, mutually beneficial sexual relationships are more likely.

Learning to channel energy and desire results in choice. Sex and pleasure can be enjoyed for their own sake and can also be transmuted into creativity and tenacity, learning how to differentiate in a way that harmonizes is part of brahmacharya.

Is it our path to bring new life into the world?

Are we using our time on earth to the maximum in a way that aligns with our own principles?

What does that look like?

How do we discern our principles?

Mindfulness around what and who we spend our energy on naturally follows.

Knowing that in human form we are necessarily limited in time and output (we only have so many years and we all need to sleep) we are awake to the dilemma of choice.

As we become clearer and more centered, it may be expected that this dilemma would dissipate. It is my experience that it only changes form and if anything, it sometimes increases.

Imagine being super clear on your principles and intentions, having a healthy body, limitless creativity and a sense of unstoppable life force within...would you want to do more or less? And as you do more, more possibilities unfold. The human feeling of so much to experience and create and so little time, is one of the forces of evolution and progress. Learning to enjoy every moment of the process is a key tenet of the yogic path and means we become present as a natural state and however hard it may be to adhere to our physical limitations in time and space, we still get to enjoy it all as we go along.

Another insight on this yama came when I began to realize the importance of having internal command over how much, how often and what I expressed in words to other people. I noticed this first when I became more aware of how other people's lack of continence was affecting my energy.

This may sound at first, to be slightly at odds with a book about clear communication though I can assure you it is probably one of the most important first steps towards it. Conscious choice around what NOT to share is an offering of respect and value to another and is not the same as withholding deep truth for fear of the response to it.

Being mindful of the mind and how many stories and judgements are constantly being made, helps us realize that what we spill onto others with our words or energy can be detrimental, especially if left unchecked.

It is easier to observe when on the receiving end.

We have all had an experience of a friend or colleague offloading their problems in our direction without our consent and of how disconcerting it can be to receive unexpected verbal outpourings from someone when we are ill-prepared to field their energy or are already having trouble maintaining our own equilibrium.

Also, when we indiscriminately purge the contents of our mind we are – by repetition - reinforcing our attachment to or belief in them - another reason to use discernment (*viveka*) in our speech.

Learning to be continent in expression and mindful of what is spoken and shared not only conserves our energy but gives us space to discern whether our communication is truthful, helpful or kind which naturally leads to more harmonious relating.

The whole system of yoga provides intelligent methods for managing our nervous system that can regulate this process through the body and help reduce obsessive and compulsive thoughts that lead to indiscriminate expression.

All this is not to say we shouldn't express negativity but rather to pay attention to how it serves us or others to do so. Sometimes a good vent or rage is refreshing after all. Is it clarifying something? Is it a chance to learn or do better next time? Or is it directionless complaining? Who feels better afterwards? Is it just you?

It is important to get the other person's agreement to receiving what you have to express in any case, especially in challenging conversations or when giving feedback – timing is everything.

It is most easy to miss all these wise suggestions when we feel out of balance ourselves. To default to emptying our mental trash onto another in words as a form of therapy is a very human habit. Although this may work on occasion (as in, may make us feel better and may be ok with the other) applying brahmacharya would suggest that, as a habit, we take the time and space necessary to regain our own equilibrium first and as often as possible, so we can once again be back in the position of feeling fully resourced and able to give rather than needing to take of another's time and energy to make ourselves feel better.

Becoming clear and aware of when you are self-sourcing and when you are taking from another is maybe one of the most profound insights into managing your own mental health, relationships and general wellbeing that you will ever find.

Acting from a more balanced perspective than when we only pursue our own gratification (although good communication is also essential in addition to right intentions.)

APARIGRAHA (NON-POSSESSIVENESS)

Parigrah means to amass, to crave or to seek or to enclose or acquire. *Graha* means to take and Pari means on all sides (and the *a* translates as a negative, meaning non.)

One of the most poignant yamas.

Being strong enough to allow people, situations and things to come in and out of your life without clinging to them is, for me, the true definition of grace.

The idea of non-attachment always held a kind of trepidation and almost a righteous anger for me, when I considered the lives of my children and others I love, and imagined I was to somehow not be attached to the content and outcome of those lives, to whether they were joyful or painful - I felt horrified, I thought it inhumane that this was expected of me.

Of course, attachment is very human and as discussed later and in a rather different context, healthy, secure attachment to other humans is a necessary trait of functional families and communities but this is different in definition to the attachment referenced here and is important to note.

Again, to get the full meaning of this yama it is necessary to explore the subtleties, so its wisdom leads to peace and wholeness rather than pain and suffering. In the Bhagavad Gita, Krishna states:

> *Let your concern be with the action alone and never with the fruits of action. Do not let the results of your action be your motive and do not be attached to inaction. ~ Bhagavad Gita*

When we worry or stress over outcomes it takes away enjoyment from the present moment. Having set ideas about the future or how others should behave is a form of clinging, sometimes another form of wanting to be right. Investing in things turning out exactly as we had envisioned reduces our capacity to roll with changes as they occur, to see the possibility in new events or to relish new experiences – instead we get disappointed or yearn for what was, which is a form of suffering. The essence of yoga is to diminish suffering and promote peace and bliss. Desperately hoping for a certain future or clinging to the past does neither of these things.

It is important here to mention that clinging is not the same as having intention (*sankalpa*).

Intention is a distinct focus for a good outcome, supported in mind and energy.

Intention contains defining qualities rather than specific results and could be understood as a gathering of one's energy towards a point rather than a grasping of any one potential outcome.

It is not possible to cling without attachment though it is possible to have a strong intention without attachment. Intention implies openness to that which is unknown while still holding space - a desire and focus - for a positive result. Clinging (*Aparigraha*) implies holding out solely for that which is desired at all costs, possibly leading to delusion and almost certainly to compromise of the present moment. When we are obsessed with a future result, the fecundity of the present moment can be invisible to us.

We cannot know the way that things are destined to turn out, we cannot know what is best for others and this realization can be very hard to take.

Letting go of people, things and situations and trusting the outcome is possibly one of the hardest lessons we will ever have to learn.

Eventually we must surrender all to death, it is inevitable, though while we are here, practicing graceful allowing is not only a form of preparation for the ending of life but it is a beautiful act of giving.

When we stop clinging to the way we imagined things should be, we don't waste valuable time wishing our lives away or berating others for not adhering to the story we had set up in our minds, instead, our awareness is renewed, and we look out with eager eyes for what will fill the empty space before us. We give ourselves back the gift of hope and anticipation and most importantly the propensity to be at peace with whatever is and to see people as free beings rather than objects in our story.

When the lives of others are entangled in our clinging and we let them (or at least their role in our story, or even the story itself) go, we are gracefully acknowledging their free will, choice and autonomy and silently removing any requirement for them to feel guilt or sadness as a result of our attachment. Energetically, this is one of the most powerful practices for resolving relating issues.

The practice of this yama has challenged me enormously and the understanding of it has also given me the greatest peace. Remembering that truth is multifaceted helps. Knowing that logic does not usually save the day and that two opposite things can both be true at the same time also helps.

Allowing everything to come and go as it must is the bravest form of grace you will ever know.

What, in your life, do you cling to?

Even if you think it is a healthy attachment, ask yourself how it would be to practice aparigraha with this particular thing, situation or person?

Might it feel lighter to swap your clinging for a broader intention?

What could that intention be?

How might the other person experience more freedom or peace were you to practice this yama?

Do you tend to cling to rightness or suffering or memories of good times? How does that impact your awareness of the here and now?

Remember we are here to experience all of it and feeling emotions and memories is part of our humanity, whereas clinging to these things has very different results than naturally experiencing them come and go.

The yamas are not another stick to beat yourself with, they are a guide to encourage peacefulness and to help us relinquish suffering. Use them accordingly.

Niyamas (restraints/observances)

SAUCHA (PURITY)

Before slipping into dangerously moralistic territory, I'd like to share a metaphor about Saucha that I found while reading on www.fragmentsofevolution.org

Categorizing anything into good and bad or clean and unclean is far too simplistic and a long way from the unity and wholeness of yoga.

Raffaello Manacorda, writing on the website above, goes on to speak about the activity of washing dishes to explain saucha.

After a meal, the dishes are cleansed with soap and water. There is nothing inherently wrong with the leftover food on the plates, it is not bad or unclean, we have eaten and been nourished by it and it can even be useful as compost. We cleanse the plates to prepare them for their next use and remove the debris before it becomes unpleasant, dries up and sticks. Understood this way, cleansing can be seen as a separating of things for different purposes.

If the purpose of yoga practice is to reduce suffering and conflict within ourselves (so this state of union and peace may exist outside of us too) it makes sense to define saucha as a categorization of those things that help us realize the essence of yoga, that support our purpose and those which do not.

One of my favorite ways of explaining yoga practice to people I teach is to describe it as a way of clearing residue from the body and mind. Washing through with the breath, aligning ourselves with our true nature and creating space for reflection all help this process of clearing.

But what about minimizing the collection of residue in our bodies and minds using Saucha as a foundational principle?

Keeping a clear, clean environment helps us function optimally in mind and is not just encouraged in yoga. The ancient Chinese philosophy of Feng Shui (closely related to Taoism) has been around for at least 3500 years as a way of harmonizing humans and life-force energy within a living environment.

Choosing nourishing, life-giving foods that help our bodies thrive rather than impede them, is another way of exercising saucha. Do you feel energetic, vital and refueled after eating and drinking or do the things you choose to put into your body leave you edgy, dulled, drained, sluggish or tired?

Choosing the thoughts that we dwell on and observing how they affect us is yet another example of how we can choose saucha.

These principles steer us in the direction of harmony and vitality and are not to be used as punishments. Evaluating how good you feel in your own life and the positive effect you have outside of yourself is the only benchmark you need employ in deciding the extent of your personal application of these principles.

Yoga is not a religion, it is a set of disciplines that will guide you toward freedom.

SANTOSHA (CONTENTMENT)

Translated as complete acceptance or satisfaction.

Years ago, when I first began to learn about yoga, santosha made me question.

How can one be content? Doesn't that mean giving up? Settling? Isn't it in conflict with some other yoga principles like sankalpa (intention) and tapas (self-discipline) that seem to infer having a goal?

It wasn't until many years later when I read Byron Katie's book – Loving What Is – that I caught a reflected light on this principle which led to one of my biggest aha moments.

Returning to one of my favorite aphorisms that seemingly contradictory statements can both be true – I understand santosha to be very much about not struggling against what is while still holding a vision of what might be.

Acceptance of reality as we perceive it can save us a whole load of heartache and time.

It does not mean that we must sacrifice our desires or relinquish intentions for more preferable scenarios in our lives, it is a firm reminder to be content and in acceptance anyway. It is a reminder that Divine timing will not be rushed or slowed and that accepting what presents itself is the smoothest way to roll in every case.

How might we do this? One of the quickest ways to naturally cultivate santosha is to get into appreciation mode. You don't even have to like it, just start listing things you appreciate, people, memories, health, privileges like a warm bed or a hot bath – many times I do this I end up in tears, it is extremely moving to bring one's awareness into this space of love. What or who do you appreciate? How many instances of beauty, connection and comfort have you experienced today? Were you to accept something that is happening now that is upsetting to you – what might be shown to you? As a friend of mine (Jamie Catto) says: If this situation had been set up specifically as a learning exercise, what would it be teaching you?

When we consider that our preferences are mostly based on incomplete perceptions and faulty conditioning, it seems less onerous to be content when things don't appear to be going our way. We never know what is around the corner. I'm reminded of the old story about the farmer whose only horse ran away, and all the villagers lamented 'oh what bad luck' and the farmer said, 'we'll see'. The next day the horse returned with 6 other wild horses and all the villagers said, 'what good luck' and the farmer said, 'we'll see'. The next day the farmer's son set off to train the wild horses but was thrown off and broke his leg, the villagers said, 'oh what bad luck' and the farmer said, 'we'll see'. Some days later, a war broke out and the Emperor's men visited the village conscripting young men for the war. The farmer's son was passed over because of his broken leg and all the villagers exclaimed 'what good luck, you must be so happy' and the farmer said 'well, we'll see'. As time went on the farmer's son's leg healed though he was left with a limp. All the other young men who had gone to war never returned and the farmer and his son were the only remaining able-bodied men who could work the land in the village. In time, the village relied on them for produce and they became very wealthy and were very generous to all the villagers. The villagers said, 'we are so fortunate, you must be very happy', the farmer smiled and said, 'we'll see'.

Standing in the knowledge that we can only know what we know at any given point in time and that there is always something hidden leaves us free to accept the potential every situation, the infinite possibility glimmering in the distance, just beyond a seemingly unsatisfactory outcome. After all, outcomes are infinite too. Our true nature is aware that although our bodies are finite, our spirit is part of a continuum and so any outcome is just the next event on a continuous wave form of happening. What goes up will come down and what fragments will rejoin.

That we have come into existence against all odds, that we breathe and live in the world, means we are already winning. We have so much to feel contented about when we zoom out of our local troubles and complaints. We do not need to diminish our local situation but rather to expand our awareness more broadly and encompass the universal that makes the local possible.

TAPAS (PERSEVERANCE/ SELF-DISCIPLINE)

The root of this Sanskrit word means 'to burn'.

The fire of tapas burns away impurities in thought and behavior that prevent us from being in the true state of yoga or union with all that is – it is sometimes translated as austerity.

Not to be confused with difficulty – tapas is more closely related to persistence or tenacity rather than purely the short term overcoming of difficult things. Continuing to do the things we've always done will get us the results we've always got – we tend to favor the things that are familiar and easy for us. Distinct changes come from attempting new things, sometimes things we don't even like – using tapas we can burn through our own reticence to start or continue a practice that we know will bring lasting benefits.

Some things in our practice are difficult but seeking to improve and master things for the sake of 'being better' misses the point. It is easy to get drawn into the ego game of surpassing personal limits and becoming really good at things – which there is nothing inherently wrong with – but making this your mission misses the point of yoga itself as the focus starts to rest on the external achievement instead of on the internal alignment that provides our peace of mind.

Staying put in difficult challenges can sometimes be character building but continuing at all costs only to prove your strength, is misguided. Coming back to tricky interactions again and again with the intention of harmony and learning is subtly different. Giving yourself sufficient recovery time is also important both physically and mentally.

In asana practice, there can be a confusion around tapas – without awareness we may push ourselves excessively to perfect a certain posture which may take time away from other important areas of our lives or injure our bodies. This is not the essence of tapas and conflicts with the overall essence of yoga. Tapas does ask that we return to our practice at some of the most difficult times, it does ask that we try one more time to see a hard situation from a new perspective and it does ask that we practice and remain in trust even when our world appears wrong and unjust. Tapas is the heat that melts through ingrained habits of body and mind that no longer serve us while staying in awareness and not veering into self-harm either.

Tapas is the fire that burns away self-doubt, victim-mode, pessimism and the thoughts we continue to think that keep us in misery. Tapas is commitment to the highest good through firm command of ourselves and perseverance even when it feels the hardest.

The outcome of practicing tapas, as with all the other limbs of yoga, is the reduction of suffering. Once we have learned, we do not habitually return to the old painful way of doing things, we may slip on occasion but that is a misstep not an unconscious pattern that has a hold over us. Practicing tapas could be seen as a motivation to keep opening to our full potential, a call to try again, to do differently, to do more. The subsequent expansion and growth reminds us we are living beings with limitless possibility. Continuing to challenge ourselves helps us operate from an awake and aware standpoint. The further we travel on our path, the more perspective we gain and the more compassion for others is available to us.

Where in your life might you use more tapas? What is your relationship with self-discipline, tenacity, perseverance? Do you tend to keep going at all costs and to your own detriment or do you use discernment to know when to move on? Are you able to drop into awareness and feel the difference between when to drop misaligned effort and when to continue in the strong heat of practice? Can you think of a challenge you overcame that gave you insight into someone else's struggle?

SVADHYAYA (STUDY OF SELF/REFLECTION)

Sva means self or belonging to me and adhyaya means enquiry or observation.

One of the best ways to begin this process of honest self-reflection is to write down your thoughts and feelings - to journal. When you return to read them after some time has passed you will be able to observe yourself as if through the eyes of another. What were once accurate representations of your inner world shape shift into a multi-layered story that holds insights and revelations. The difficulty of using one's own mind to observe one's own mind is perhaps one of the most challenging aspects of both knowing ourselves and relating with others - that we can only notice our blind spots in retrospect.

Adopting the position of observer or witness becomes essential for honest evaluation.

It is, at first, hard to remain in witness consciousness without becoming self-conscious about how we express ourselves. Watching oneself is odd until it becomes normal. Restricting the natural, beautiful human element of letting life flow through us without impediment and letting it move us in the ways we speak and act, is not the aim. To never make a mistake is not the aim.

Study of the self includes all aspects of self, our human, our body and our higher self, the things we like about our humanness and the things we don't, the unchanging nature of our true nature and how we tune into it.

Notice the translation includes enquiry rather than just observation – this denotes a curiosity that can refresh our direction when we become stuck in patterns that aren't working. It's not usually a question of why we behave like we do but more a question of how. How do we do what we do? What happens when we do it that way? How might things go differently? Why tends to lead backwards and is often less than helpful – how tends to move us closer to solutions and insights and feels more rounded and less judgmental.

Observing the body is a powerful way of dropping into awareness about ourselves. Our bodies are constantly delivering wisdom to us in the form of subtle sensations that can bring us into closer communion with our wholeness and help us understand the how of our process. Seeing as what happens in the mind affects the body and vice versa, it is possible to access parts of our consciousness that would otherwise be hidden to us if we enquire via the body rather than using the analytical, logical route that has enjoyed such praise since Freud and the beginning of the talking therapies trend.

We are seeing a shift now toward holistic interpretation of ourselves with the advancement of medical technology such as fMRI machines leading to an increased awareness of how memory and impactful events are stored in our bodies not only in our minds. Watching the body unfold through asana practice is another important way of studying how past events have shaped us, where we hold blocks or tensions and how we can gently begin to dissolve old traumas and come into alignment once more with our true nature.

To live from our truth requires learning to drop inhibition and habits that don't serve us but also to review our behaviors and relationships with awareness.

Having courage enough to repair harm where we have caused it (as we invariably will at some point) is using svadhayaya for good and helps our minds collate encouraging evidence that we are in alignment with our higher self and do indeed have the power to bring about positive change.

With practice, svadhyaya starts to become automatic in our daily lives. Tuning into and reflecting on our true nature on a regular basis acts as a guide for right action. Tuning into our humanness helps us have compassion for ourselves and others and provides valuable feedback for learning and connection.

Do you reflect on your behavior? When you reflect on the quality of your connections with others, how do you see your role in these? In what ways do you make space for regular tuning in and observation of self?

ISVARAPRANIDHARA (CONTEMPLATION OF AND SURRENDER TO SUPREME CONSCIOUSNESS)

Ishvara means to dedicate or surrender. Pranidhara is a name for God or the Ultimate Reality.

Sometimes called surrender to love or offering of self to the Way – this final Niyama is a call to inhabit our higher self, our true nature and let the complexities of the mind and emotions be seen from a distance, knowing that we are more than our bodies and minds only.

This kind of surrender is not a giving up, it is a trust. It is an offering.

The yoga Sutra this comes from (2.45) states:

Perfection and liberation come from aligning oneself with the highest intelligence.

Opening our perception to include everything that we know we could never know – the extent of the Universe, how we got here, what other people experience or all that our lives will include – brings with it a sense of awe that can only be described as holy.

When we recall the divinity housed within us, it becomes natural to express it in gratitude, service, joy and creativity. This contemplation of all that is can bring us to a desperate nihilism if we refuse to see ourselves as a part of it. Drops of water make up the ocean.

The tightrope line between overwhelming insignificance and profound awe takes heartfelt practice to walk. We fall off either side. Ishvara Pranidhana asks us to keep surrendering to practice, keep attuning our lives to our true nature, keep remembering when we forget.

We are all part of this unfathomable Divinity, no-one is excluded – not even those who have forgotten and have done unspeakable things.

In your remembering of who you truly are, you become a force for good, you remember for those who have forgotten and in doing so, become a proponent for union in every single relationship you will ever have. Relationships make up families, communities and nations. Your remembering and your practice of yoga in whatever form it may take, becomes a balm for the scrapes and painful scratches of being human. Your willingness to use yoga principles to inform your way of being increases the likelihood of harmonious communication and a strong sense of mutual connection that is the very foundation for peace.

CHAPTER 4
THE LIMBS OF YOGA

Asana (posture) & Pranayama

(breath awareness)

I t feels sensible to put these two limbs of yoga together as both asana and pranayama have become the most recognizable features of yoga in the modern age and are the final two limbs that are primarily focused on the body. Maybe the powerful effects on wellbeing and mental health that can be achieved by practicing only these two limbs have made this so, for the results are indeed undeniable.

I am fascinated by neuroscience and physiology and love learning the scientific data that supports the efficacy of yoga.

I attended the Yoga & The Mind conference in London a few years ago wanting to hear the worldly evidence of what I knew to be true in my own mind and body. I

wanted more language to describe and explain my experience to those who didn't already know it for themselves.

A selection of eminent neuroscientists, doctors and yogis all gathered to speak about the most recent findings linking yoga asana and pranayama (and meditation) with good mental health, alleviation of symptoms and recovery from trauma.

People from Harvard, Boston teaching hospital, India and the UK presented for 2 days all the evidence-based research they had collated using western medicine's technologies and parameters. Through rich and diverse information, it became clear how powerful yoga can be as an intervention. From depression to PTSD, the effects of yoga versus medication were measured and tested. The results were heartening.

(Due to the hugeness of this topic which is gathering more momentum every day and to stay on point I will present this information as it relates to conscious connection and include further research and resources in the notes.)

ASANA

The movement and placement of the body in specific positions and sequences as part of a yoga practice. Asana brings physical benefits to all the systems of the body including flexibility and strength.

Digging deeper, where management of mind is understood to be one of the key components in living well and when we understand how past trauma and experiences leave an imprint in the body, we recognize the comprehensive purpose and benefit of asana as a healing modality.

Acknowledging areas of sensitivity and damage through mindful movement (and pranayama) aids the safe release and integration of past pain or injury and effectively takes us back to neutral - a pre-requisite for developing and strengthening sustainably.

Knowing one's own body and feeling safe there is essential in connecting with others and helps us manage our state with discernment and observe others with compassion during challenging interactions.

Yoga therapy and experience in subtle body anatomy enables incisive readings of a person's emotional and energetic patterns just from the way they carry themselves. A stability of self arises from attunement with our physicality that can reduce tendencies to blame and judge others and help us remain steady despite difficulties.

Add to this the massive impact that physical bodily adjustments and changes have on the physiology and function of the brain and we see the important role of this specific type of bodily discipline.

VAGUS NERVE AND BREATHING WELL

The vagus nerve carries information from body to brain and brain to body though not in equal measure.

Eighty percent (approx.) of the signals carried by this nerve are 'bottom up' signals or from the body to the brain. Exhaling long and deeply stimulates the vagus and sends messages to the brain to activate the parasympathetic nervous system – or the part that prepares the body for resting, digesting and sexual activity.

Using the body, we command the body.

There are things that our conscious brain can't normally command and controlling certain aspects of the body's autonomic functioning is one of them. Breathing well unlocks this capability.

The vagus has tendrils running from the head all the way down to the pelvis.

Speaking to the subconscious via the body can short circuit the most deeply held habits and change how our nervous system responds.

Accessing the body to change the brain and thus effect our mind and emotions is a valuable part of both asana and pranayama.

Mindful breathing (pranayama) can slow the heart rate and regulate heart rate variability (which is a marker of good health and longevity).

The more we practice using specific areas of the brain, the more they develop, much like training muscles in the body. Synapses that fire together more often, make stronger neural pathways. What does this mean for us? If we practice relaxation it becomes physically easier for us to access this as a state of being.

Remembering that our true nature, our spirit – is housed in this body, it is timely to speak of the energetic centers of the body – in Yoga, named chakras (wheels).

Throughout the world, the location of such energetic pathways in the body is more or less agreed on, though the names may differ. They relate to specific points where energy and matter meet.

Meridians (in TCM) nadis (in Yoga) and the central channel that follows the spine (or that the spine follows?) named Sushumna, have all been utilized for thousands of years to provide forms of healing such as acupuncture, shiatsu and reflexology to name a few.

Some of these points relate to the health of the major organs and can be used in diagnosis and stimulation to bring back balance and health.

A good asana practice allows the spine to move in all the ways it was designed to and calms and stimulates all the major organs as well as exercising the muscles, manipulating the connective tissue and strengthening the ligaments to provide basic support for the skeleton. These processes also have a chemical and hormone effect that further changes the whole system.

Considering what we already know about how the health of the body affects the mind, it is easy to see how asana and pranayama practice can bring immediate benefit by creating feel good chemicals and normalizing the major functions like heart rate, temperature and digestion.

In addition to this, if we regularly bring awareness to our bodies, we recognize accumulation of tension and stagnation as it arises. We can look at the subtle body clues and consider how our balance may be restored in body or mind. Often, when one is attuned very closely, it is possible to spot problems before they become serious illness.

If we are thorough in shifting issues as they arise we can rebalance with appropriate changes and dedicated practice and are more able to take on new information and challenges of all types with a clearer perspective.

Respecting the body as our vehicle for this life contributes to our health, strength, self-worth and clarity of expression. When we feel good we can do good.

When we have the clarity that a well-maintained body and mind afford us, there is less reactivity and when there is less reactivity we create less karma (and less drama) for ourselves and others).

This whole process fashions us into vessels that can allow life force to flow through us – less acclimatized to clinging and more used to flowing, accepting change as it occurs and becoming flexible of mind as well as body. We develop as clear conduits that life can express itself through and in so doing are able to channel this energy with more agency.

Relating from this empowered and physically rooted stance is different and although we still require communication tools, this attention to the body through physical practice gives the foundation for the next level of practice.

PRATYAHARA

Often translated as 'withdrawal of the senses' – this limb is named from *'prati'* meaning against and *'ahara'* meaning nourishment, food or anything external that is taken into ourselves.

Considering what we allow into our experience on a regular basis is one of the most important factors in setting good boundaries. Boundaries can be more usefully seen, not as restrictions but more as containers. If our aim is to focus and direct our energy toward the outcomes we intend and the qualities of service we wish to embody and offer, then it makes sense that we spend less time and energy deflecting that which prevents us from this.

To be efficient with our energy, we make choices about what we allow into our field because of the way it impacts on our energy usage.

Filtering with discernment (viveka) can be an efficiency and saves time.

As an example, if I watch or read the news regularly and feel helpless and depressed about the state of the world, it will take me more time to reinstate my equilibrium and gather my energy sufficiently that I can direct it towards creativity, service or simply feeling good. When I realize the effect watching the news is having on me and compare it to how I function when I limit this activity, I realize that I am happier, more positive and generally more able to contribute positively when I exercise pratyahara. This is not the same as living in a bubble. Having awareness of something is different to putting yourself purposefully in the path of something and being oblivious to its effect on you and by extension, on others. As another example, if water was limited and you wanted to keep yourself clean, it would be silly to get yourself dirty unnecessarily.

To understand any of these principles, it is essential to realize our own agency and the potential for impact we have on others. To deny this equates to a lack of responsibility or at the very least a willful ignorance regarding our own power. To embrace it gives access to and consciousness of our otherwise latent potential for creating positive outcomes.

In what other ways might we exercise pratyahara?

What we take in either encourages or discourages our intentions, feeds or depletes our bodies and spirits and helps clarify or clutter our minds. What we eat, talk about, listen to, read, watch and expose ourselves to, all leaves an imprint on us which requires integrating in some way.

It would be easy to become ultra-purist on contemplation of pratyahara and indeed, some do choose that route. It can seem simpler to remove anything that appears to cause disruption to our notions of ourselves.

I prefer to hone my awareness by continuing to expand my experience – not necessarily restricting what comes in but keeping strong discernment as to what effect it has on me and weighing up whether the agitation is a sign of newness and maturation or destructiveness. This is important in human relating – are the fractious, jarring interactions a necessary redirect to previously unseen truth or are they a perpetual whittling away at our energy that leaves us depleted and lacking in resources?

Balance is essential to all living things.

Knowing what helps you thrive and what hinders your growth, expansion and enjoyment is key to realizing balance and having a strategy for restoring it each time it is lost. Mindful attention towards what we allow into our orbit can help us conserve valuable energy and focus while preventing time-wasting self sabotage. As with all things – practice provides clarity and experience guides us toward a deep internal knowing.

As you consider your daily routine, at what points do you feel the most energized, inspired and creative? Do you associate a particular activity to these states? Conversely – are there things you read, watch or listen to (including people) that leave you drained, tired and lethargic? What might it look like if you developed a new, energy-conserving boundary in your life? What do you take in through your senses that nourishes you? Is there room for more of this?

DHARANA (FOCUSSED CONCENTRATION)

Translated as 'holding', 'holding steady' or 'single focus'.

Fixing our full attention on one place requires phenomenal discipline.

With the torrents of information flooding our systems every day via screens, maintaining single focus for any length of time can seem more and more difficult. But there are times when we are naturally able to do this, and it does not feel at all like effort. The state of flow we experience when engaged in creativity, nature or mindful physical movement is a special kind of concentration that feels very different to trying to solve a hard maths equation or read a complex book. Developing dharana may contribute to what

Jason Silva calls 'hacking the flow state'. The more we practice holding a steady focus, the easier it becomes to drop into this state of awareness and be present. To hold steady in single pointed attention is not only to powerfully gather your energy and will but also to be in a state of keen observation of self – beyond the mind and body.

Mindfulness is essentially the practice of developing dharana.

Concentrating attention on the now, being fully engaged with this moment – is one of the major differences between conscious and unconscious relating.

When we exercise dharana, we can more readily differentiate between what is fleeting, what is past memory and future projection and what is integral and unchanging. In the process we get to know the authentic self in its truest form and stretch our capacity to move fluidly from one moment to the next with less attachment and expectation. The beauty of dharana, when practiced with intent, is that it increases our capacity for holding or 'having-ness' -the more we focus and figuratively sit still, the more we expand our ability to be, in a state of equilibrium, with whatever is presenting at the time, firstly from our own psyche and then from external events.

In this way we become more adept at being with all manner of reactions that arise from our interacting with life and we subsequently can augment the skill and dexterity required to handle the reactions of others too.

Working with this knowledge of who we truly are and being able to streamline our internal resources is the foundation of any and all achievements ever made – this is what enables great poets and artists to create, explorers to explore and mathematicians to solve complex problems that change our perspective of reality.

The ability to manage and command an otherwise scattered mind while also being aligned with your deepest inner knowing, is the first step toward realizing any outcome that is wished for.

In relating, there are times when it is necessary and kind to hold space for another while they recalibrate or gather their resources, something we will only be able to recognize the need for and manage, when we are au fait with holding space and steady attention for and by ourselves. Sometimes it is necessary to hold space for others to ease our own process too – being able to stay neutral in the face of someone else's reactions is a mighty strength that can open the door to deep insights. When we are better equipped to remain in our own integrity and steadiness from regular practice of dharana, it is easier to hear our internal guidance, to listen the wisdom of our bodies and to maintain mental and emotional balance when it is most necessary. It is also easier to see how our individual dramas play out without taking it so personally.

Balance gives perspective and power – it can take the heat out of fiery altercations and diminish hurtful outbursts. Using a physical analogy, think of trying to absorb a blow to the body without crumpling while standing on one leg versus when you have both feet firmly on the ground and muscles engaged – dharana is like the strong, engaged stance that provides steadiness and strength no matter what we encounter.

Trying to communicate well with someone who is distracted, volatile or unsteady is like trying to hit a moving target while dodging bullets – challenging, disconcerting and almost guaranteed to trigger a stress response. Imagine attempting to share deeply held feelings with a person that is unable to sit with their own yet? Imagine trying to communicate well when either or both parties are in the midst of a huge fight/flight/freeze reaction where all capacity for reasoning has shut down and only black or white thinking remains...Yet many of us try in desperation and then wonder why, instead of connection, conflict arises. Dharana gives us the ability to remain focused without becoming consumed by external events.

This limb of practice is where we acknowledge and accept what is, allow any residue to surface and release, make internal space and gain clarity for ourselves. This holding steady equates to being with ourselves for long enough that we can discern what is surface and what is innate.

Focus of this kind can bring a tenacity and staying power that prevails much longer than the initial burst of enthusiasm for a course of action may last because our energy is not split. When we are not fighting ourselves internally or scattering our focus on multiple thoughts and distractions - we have more energy to spare. When we have the focus to sit with ourselves in full awareness, we become steadily surer of our intentions.

Dharana essentially strengthens our ability to stay present and gives momentum to our intentions whilst also helping us to remain awake to the subtle cues that suggest a change in direction.

Mastery of the mind starts here and is the perfect preparation for limb number seven – Dhyana.

DHYANA (MEDITATIVE ABSORPTION)

Profound meditation. From *dhyai* – to think of.

In Patanjali's Yoga Sutras, meditation is defined as 'when the mind has been able to transcend the knowledge of smell, sound, touch, form and taste, and at the same time, when the consciousness is functioning around one point'.

What happens when you remain in steady focus but remove the object of your attention? Be it a candle flame, a thought or an interaction? What is left?

If, while glimpsing our source during dharana, energy and intention has become organized around an object, then dhyana is the all-encompassing stillness that gives space for this source to become known by us, to be recognized, a space to commune with our very essence. This state of meditation sometimes resembles prayer – not in the religious sense of asking for something but as a most profound emptiness that is akin to deep listening.

In this stillness, attachments subside, thought slows and fades, the fascination with form naturally falls away and is replaced with the effortless realization of how everyone and everything is interconnected. It is only in this state that we can gain a perspective that does not depend on external reality as perceived through our filters.

To be willing to not cling to thought or form and to let our expectations dissolve, requires surrender. It makes sense then that this is the penultimate limb in the eight-fold path. After we have become acquainted with all the trappings of humanity and the many tools we can use to alleviate our suffering, we finally begin earnest preparation for the end goal of integration and the realization that all we are aware of now will end.

This practice of real yoga and the willingness to enter into human relating with the same reverence eventually strips us of all our illusions. This is death practice. All our conditioning, all our human instincts draw us to attachment, back to any facsimile of the pre-birth state - harmony and timeless bliss, the formless omnipresence of love. Yet the semi-conscious knowledge that we are divine, spiritual beings is intractably tangled up with the reality of being human and finite – we are going to die.

How do we resolve dying when our true nature and spirit is forever – like the universe – no beginning and no end? How do we reconcile this painful paradox without fragmenting ourselves? How can we live knowing that at some point we must surrender in death? More to the point – how could we not do our absolute utmost to love every valuable moment and nurture each precious connection in the light of this?

To know that we are divine and at the same time human necessitates making room for every seemingly opposite truth. On this axis of awareness is where duality meets oneness.

The eight-fold path provides a complete system for keeping our balance in between the paradox of inevitable heart-stopping awe (everything matters) and complete nihilism (nothing matters) that is generated by this awareness.

Dhyana is the backdrop of peace where disparate disputes of mind and spirit can fall away. In the quiet understanding that there are elements of truth in everything, we become acquainted with the responsibility of choice – of choosing which truths we wish to focus on and thus how we want to feel and what contributions we can offer into the world.

SAMADHI (ENLIGHTENMENT/UNION WITH THE DIVINE)

Samadhi means putting together or integration, ecstasy with the Divine

This was the most challenging aspect of yoga to describe with words.

In compelling linear terms, this is it, the end of the practice, the mystical finale.

Described by some as death of the ego or a moment of enlightenment from which point everything changes or the moment of physical death. How can we understand what samadhi is?

A good friend – also a teacher of consciousness – described samadhi as the state which lies underneath everything. I understood this well. Our true nature is divine and as such cannot be experienced through the 5 senses so is necessarily troublesome to describe using language.

Vedanta names our true nature Brahman or the Atman – the Ultimate Reality that is underneath the ever-changing universe and the soul which refers to the part of that which is within each of us. The quality of this is Ananda – bliss or peace that is present even amidst great outer turmoil.

When there is no resistance to anything, when thoughts are merely observed like passing clouds, when the realization of our oneness with all that is, happens – this is samadhi as I understand it.

Meditative states can give fleeting experiences of samadhi. Meditation is like listening out for samadhi, making quiet space for it to appear. Communing with this part of ourselves which is part of all that is, is so powerful – it is the energy that creates worlds – aligning ourselves with it brings natural harmony to our human experience and increases our access to intuition and flow states. Awareness of this underlying peace is the ultimate experience of union.

CHAPTER 5
ATTACHMENT THEORY

Relational awareness and non-duality

A pivotal step in linking the conditioning received in early years to adult patterns of relational behavior is Attachment Theory. With all the yoga wisdom and knowledge of self in the world, even the sincerest attempts at harmonious connection can still fall flat if our communication skills are inadequate.

Defining a way of being in the world that is understood gives us so much more power to effect positive change around us.

Effective relations with others happen when we take full responsibility for our communication, which incorporates how we understand others and how we are understood. Learning what mental filters we are using helps us be better equipped to navigate any kind of communication. As an added benefit, when we discern what kind of attachment style and filters others are using, we are instinctually more patient and compassionate because we have better understanding.

First introduced by John Bowlby, a British psychologist, psychiatrist and psychoanalyst born in 1907, (who was, not incidentally, brought up primarily by a nanny) this theory provides important foundations to the complex subject of adult human relating.

Because the relationship between an infant and the primary caregiver shapes the infant's own sense of self so significantly, it is from here that we begin and from here that we can start to understand the dynamics of every other relationship we go on to have.

Our natural state is one of secure attachment.

In the field of psychology, attachment is seen as the foundation of our psychological life. John Bowlby (1982), the originator of attachment theory, proposed that for a child, the attachment bond with a protective, loving adult figure is a primary mechanism for the maintenance and regulation of safety.

The caregiver serves as a secure base (Ainsworth et al., 1978) and is crucial in promoting the child's experience of safety and connectedness. (from Fosha, 2000). Therefore, how we attach early in life is an extremely important aspect of human development. Our attachment patterns affect us throughout all areas and phases of life. They determine how well we can be in relationship and how well we cope with stress.

> *"The attachment system is active "from cradle to grave. . . when a person is distressed, ill or afraid." (Bowlby, 1977, p. 203).*

Bowlby was heavily influenced by Donald Winnicott, an English pediatrician whose work with children and mothers led to his influential concept of the "holding environment". Winnicott saw that secure and safe holding as provided by the primary caregiver helped the infant experience their own body as a safe place and furthermore, this concept of a "holding environment" expanded to other social settings the child went on to encounter in addition to the parent-child dynamic. When adequately provided, this holding environment contributed to the child's healthy development. Where this did not take place adequately enough in childhood, different styles of attachment were more likely to form – classified under three broad categories as Anxious, Avoidant and Disorganized.

(It is now widely accepted that a therapist may provide the "holding space" for an adult in retrospect, to support important internal changes and healing of early childhood experience)

It is interesting to me that a common phrase in spiritual self-help and yoga circles is that of "holding space" for others, my understanding of which is very much aligned with the explanation put forward by Winnicott – that of providing an energetic bed, without resistance or influence, that can hold emotion and expression securely enough and for long enough that the giver of these can observe and remain in the vicinity of them without feeling overwhelmed.

This process of holding (safe) space is vital as a healing tool, especially for those who tend to intellectualize that which is emotionally charged (rather than re-feel it) or who avoid or ignore the physical signals that there is a psycho-emotional disturbance requiring their attention or who use non-dual wisdom as a means of avoiding relational healing.

Holding space encompasses both the invitation to view what is happening from a different perspective and to experience being with difficult emotions originating from childhood in a safe space.

Until we can somatically experience this sense of safety in the presence of another at the same time as recalling trauma (which equates to re-experiencing the trauma in our minds and bodies), the survival instinct pushes us toward the tendency to keep avoiding this pain. To begin the delicate work of addressing childhood trauma anew with the expanded capabilities of the adult involves both psychological and somatic attention of the highest quality, in other words – sometimes we need help.

> John Welwood states, "The hard truth is that spiritual realizations often do not heal our deep wounding...most modern spiritual practitioners continue to act out unconscious relational patterns developed in childhood. Often what is needed here is psychological work that allows us to bring the underlying psychodynamics that maintain these patterns in to consciousness."

There is plentiful information regarding the effects of trauma and adverse childhood experiences on the brain and body. Neuroscience and medical investigations are rapidly defining the details of our psycho-emotional processing or lack of and its correlation to our physical bodies. The link between brain and body has never been so widely accepted. Physical alterations in size and shape of brain areas is a known side effect of trauma and has far-reaching consequences on the ability to reason, relax and connect unless addressed. Evidence-based research supporting what ancient traditions have known for eons keeps growing steadily.

It is important to clarify here that the definition of trauma in this context includes any happening or relational dynamic that the child perceives as a threat. It is not only the children of addicts, abusers and neglectful parents that develop harmful coping mechanisms. It is not just exposure to war zones, violence or horror that impacts on attachment style and emotional development. Anything that causes a significant enough physical fear response in the body can trigger a psychological change that affects future perception and behaviors, especially if no reassurance is available for the child following the instance or series of instances. Children with acute psychic and emotional sensitivities are most significantly affected.

For example, insecure attachment can follow an early life of the caregiver providing very well for the child's physical needs while simultaneously disregarding or preventing emotional connection and closeness. It is common to justify and rationalize early impactful experiences simply because we have awareness of something much worse happening to others.

Going even deeper into the physicality of such events – we now know that the brain's physiology is subject to change depending on which areas of it are utilized. This phenomenon known as neuroplasticity is one of the reasons that yoga and meditation practices have the potential for sustainable and deep-seated change of the individual. We know that trauma in the early years can prevent certain areas of the brain from developing but also that coordinated mind-body practices (specifically yoga) that includes controlled breathing – can stimulate new growth of neurons and synapses and develop key areas of the brain that did not develop fully in childhood, even increasing grey matter.

TYPES OF ATTACHMENT

> *Our brains are genetically hard-wired for attachment. The brain's attachment system directs us to seek connection and closeness from the beginning of life. This connection is needed in order to structure our brain for healthy relationships and well-being. (Badenoch, 2008)*

Bowlby defined three major types of attachment style that are adaptive i.e. derive from destabilization or trauma.

Anxious, Avoidant/Dismissive and Disorganized, suggesting that most people exhibit tendencies of all three styles in their search for secure attachment in intimate relationships. (I am including family members in the term "intimate relationships")

"No matter how much insight and understanding we develop, the rational brain is basically impotent to talk the emotional brain out of its own reality" ~ Bessel van der Kolk – The Body Keeps The Score

INDEPENDENCE. DEPENDENCE. INTERDEPENDENCE.

In a healthy society, family or relationship, the capacity for independence, dependence and interdependence make for harmony, cohesiveness and strength. Being dependent on someone for something is a marker of our ability to make agreements, to understand coherently (one side of connection) and to trust. Being independent is necessary for taking action, for realizing the things that align with our inner knowing and creatively expressing. Interdependence is the beautiful state of comprehending we are all connected, we all have impact on each other and we all need each other.

A quick review of how those states are created and reinforced in childhood goes a long way to explaining relating styles in adulthood.

Object constancy develops around 18 months – this comes from the experience of reliability, the knowing that when mum or dad leaves the room, they will come back again in more or less the same form.

Object permanence = continuity – knowing that an object still exists even when it cannot be seen/heard/felt.

Disruption to the child's sense of secure attachment comes from on/off parenting and responsiveness when the feeling of constancy or reliability is diminished. This can stem from if a parent is unpredictable or unreliable in their availability or mood then the child's internal experience is one of inconsistency/unpredictability which manifests as anxiety. Big experiences like moving home, going to boarding school, sudden deaths and illnesses all impact the delicate family dynamic and thus the growing child as they develop their sense of self.

(It is important to note that a few occasions of being in a bad mood are unlikely to have lasting effects on a child's development. Winnicott coined the phrase "good enough parenting" which is worth reading about if you want reassurance.)

Let's consider some of the defining characteristics of each attachment style to further understand how they can exhibit in a relational dynamic.

Once we understand how attachment systems manifest, it becomes easier to ascertain how we interact with them (almost thinking of it as separate from the person can help) and how to soothe the nervous system when it has been triggered into a reaction that stems from past pain. It is only from a generally relaxed place that authentic connection between two parties can flower unimpeded. In Diane Poole Heller's book 'Healing Your Attachment Wounds', she emphasizes the need to acknowledge and tend to the attachment system as a priority so that healing can happen, and compensating behaviors can reduce. Healing of any kind does not imply that the original trauma is forgotten or fixed but rather that it no longer controls our lives.

Most people have some elements of more than one attachment style. The more fully developed and uninterrupted our attachment systems had chance to be in childhood, the more we tend towards secure attachment in adulthood. In times of great challenge or stress even the most securely attached will fall back on behaviors borne out of stress responses in childhood (known as Attachment Adaptation.)

Having the awareness to recognize and deal well with such periods of temporary regression makes the difference between exacerbating existing emotional and mental blind spots and illuminating them for what they are – residue of past painful experiences.

Once we shine light on the shadow it loses its power over us.

These lists are not exhaustive and recognizing some of the listed traits does not automatically signify incapability of secure attachment. Being able to identify tendencies reduces confusion and helps us act with understanding and compassion.

ANXIOUS ATTACHMENT

Causes: When the parents were either anxious attachers themselves or were unable to provide a safe port so that the child felt able to explore and return safely. Parents were often inconsistent in mood/behavior or their presence could not be relied upon.

Some characteristics of people with anxious attachment tendencies are as follows:

Attempt to stabilize the connection by over-talking.

Over-function or over-give to accommodate others.

Fear of loss.

Over-focus on others and lose selves in relationship.

Hard to say no or set boundaries.

Second guess self, feel insecure.

Give more than they get and feel resentful.

Difficult to receive love.

Hard to be alone.

Stressed, abandoned, hurt or angry when alone.

Picking fights after absences.

Merge into partner and feel their feelings – prioritize over own.

Need reassurance.

Stress on leaving (separation anxiety)

Need to be in close proximity with loved ones.

AVOIDANT/DISMISSIVE ATTACHMENT

Causes: When parents were either absent, rejecting or not very present with the child or only when they were task focused.

Some characteristics of people with this attachment style are as follows:

Emotionally unavailable.

Minimize the importance of close relations.

Insist on self-reliance, find it hard to reach out for help.

Do most things alone – feel (hurtfully) superior because of this.

Eye contact is uncomfortable.

Easier to think rather than feel.

Initially feel elated when relationship ends then feel depressed when realizing it might be over for good. (Don't take it personally)

Workaholic.

Dismiss own needs or are unaware of them.

Abnormally self-sufficient to the point of not honoring or respecting others' needs.

Original relationship template was formed around isolation.

Unaware of the level of disconnection – attachment system is switched off/shut down.

Stop feeling the need for connection.

No feeling of wanting to share or talk about emotions - feels unnatural.

Stress/anxiety on approach.

Hard to engage in joint attention.

Not expressing commitment.

Appearance of devaluing the relationship.

DISORGANISED ATTACHMENT

Causes: Child suffered loss or multiple changes in caregiver before 3yrs. Parents suffered loss or trauma or were frightening or frightened around the child. This is the most insecure type of attachment.

Some tendencies of people who attach in this way are as follows:

Dissociative behaviors/psychopathology.

Lacks a coherent style of coping with challenge.

Becomes easily overwhelmed.

Negative self-concepts.

Complex PTSD can develop if disruption is significant.

Once we illuminate the old programs running our current interactions, it is both empowering and clarifying and the first step in taking ownership of our part in any dynamic with another person.

TRIGGERED

Attachment adaptations become underlying mental programs that are etched into our subconscious. They do not have to be permanent though it is required to acknowledge them if we do not want them in control of our minds and relationships.

Understanding what to do when we or someone else gets triggered is one of the most important factors in being able to manage and repair a relationship of any kind. The phrase 'the presenting problem is not really the problem' sums up triggered in a nutshell.

When our subconscious beliefs and programs are activated by a comment or action in the present moment, it can be difficult for even us to know what happened to provoke such a heightened reaction - for others it can be impossible.

Not acknowledging felt pain or anger can lead to relationship breakdown, as can total disengagement when things get too confusing or fractious. How do we soothe activated nervous systems and promote healthy adaptation at the same time?

Considering attachment styles helps us first understand the trigger points and second, know how best to attempt repair of the connection. For instance, an anxious attacher may find it extremely stressful if the other party needs to retreat from the connection after an argument, the retreat may be the most sensible option to prevent further damage but if not communicated adequately will probably be perceived as abandonment. Conversely, for an avoidant attacher insistence on 'having it out' there and then, or 'getting to the bottom of it' to resolve matters would likely feel claustrophobic and too overwhelming to the point that they become unable to access their resources and go into a kind of shutdown from which space no effective collaboration can take place.

The subconscious and the nervous system work very well to protect our interests – they want to always save us from pain or harm. Until we bring light to what is unconscious and make it conscious, we are always going to keep struggling against automatic defenses in any challenging situation. When we become aware of our conditioned responses, communicate clearly and practice being at the edge of our capabilities (where we are just safe enough to broach the unknown or potentially scary) all kinds of wonders occur.

Firstly, we start to know what we are truly capable of.

Secondly, we begin to make choices about the type of people and circumstances we want to make ourselves available for – in other words – we define our edge, for now.

Are we experiencing newness and healthy challenge or persistent damage that makes us contract? In a growing, learning, evolving human, the edge is always changing, in my experience as a woman, our edge changes with our cycle too – some days we are sensitive, yin and soft and some days we are feisty, strong and ready to be pushed. Being present is essential to determine where your edge lies at any given moment and to act with honor to that information.

Thirdly, we develop what Ram Dass calls 'unbearable compassion'.

We see others in their humanity and their divinity. We realize that the way they get triggered or trigger us is from a residue of pain and our hearts open to that. Taking things personally becomes less habitual. We become more accustomed to looking for and finding, the essence underneath the human drama.

CHAPTER 6
INTEGRATION AND
COMMUNICATION

Once the potential power contained in this information for more accurately translating relationship dramas has landed – and it can feel like a bolt of lightning if this is the first time you've encountered it – how do we use it in day to day management of self and relating? What does conscious relating feel like?

I want to liken the difference between a conscious relationship and an unconscious one to the difference between parenting babies and late teenagers...in the beginning, you don't know yourself yet (as a parent), you do the best you can with very little actual knowledge and you muddle through. It is exhausting.

When the child reaches late teenage years, the tasks of feeding, bathing, changing and rushing to answer their every cry are no longer required. Older children require more emotional support, guidance and still love, of course.

Now you know yourself (as a parent) the pace is different, the challenges are more varied and the awareness that you are impacting an actual human being may feel stronger now they are able to communicate with you.

You have a certain confidence in yourself, you recognize the parent part of you, you see all actions through the eyes of love – your love for your child.

Conscious relating is not a blissful paradise where everyone is in harmony all the time. Like advanced parenting, just because you love your offspring does not mean they will never upset or annoy you. But parenting requires the unconditional love that says, I will love you no matter what you do. I do not expect you to stop me feeling bad. I do not expect you to solve my problems for me. If you want to stay connected with me there are some boundaries to be adhered to – respect and kindness and maybe some others. Can you see how a strong knowledge of self, a deep practice of keeping oneself clear can naturally lead to relating that is not loaded with expectation?

What a gift.

Becoming super clear on our motivations in our dealings with others is to understand the subtext of our communications.

What are we really looking for? Asking for? Wanting? Where are we still attempting to self-soothe a deep lack from childhood?

When we consider the patterning left by our early experiences and are prepared to be honest with ourselves about our strategies and behaviors, huge epiphanies are possible, shifts that can dramatically alter the quality of results we are getting. Though it's compelling to read the lists above and go around assessing the attachment style of everyone we are or have ever been close with in the hope that this will solve all our problems, this in itself will not be useful without first shining the light on your own process (believe me, I've tried it.)

HOW CAN THIS INFORMATION BE USED IN CONJUNCTION WITH THE EIGHT-FOLD PATH AS A MEANS TOWARD HARMONY AND THE REDUCTION OF SUFFERING?

The way I see it, I can be completely at peace within when I'm alone. Unchallenged. This is ok if I want to live on a mountain, on my own. I don't. Most of us want to thrive within community, to relate with others well and be resilient to challenge when it occurs and be able to mend relationships and connections when they break down. This resilience enables us to be a functioning and contributing member of humanity. This ability is key to our sense of meaning. Without it, life can get too much to bear very quickly.

Yoga is a manual for managing and maintaining the human self to the highest standard, to stay in alignment with the true nature as far as is possible. Attachment theory – when grounded in other basic, modern psychological concepts – gives a translation dictionary with which to understand our own and other people's mental programming around relating better.

Using this translation tool along with the principles of yoga, enables us to partake and to offer, nuanced communication that benefits all and feels warm and rich. Without translation tools, we rely on the goodness of intention. And sometimes magic does happen and sometimes even the best of intentions will not save a relationship between people that love each other if they cannot find a way of seeing and healing the residue of conditioning and adapting accordingly.

Adaptation has ensured our survival so far and is key to growth and sustainability. Adaptation can take place without sacrificing our intrinsic sense of self, it is a capability that helps us, a natural element of all living beings, not an undesirable option we have to use when we can't get our own way.

We suffer when we cling to an imaginary version of what is, an internal story we have of the way things ought to be. Using yoga along with conscious communication, instances of relating become arenas for development and expansion. When we are awake to where we came from (our past conditioning) we have the capacity to be honest about what is required from ourselves to get to where we want to go. Staying conscious about our interactions diminishes the tendency to blame others and get stuck in self-pity which is a version of what Byron Katie calls 'arguing with reality' – an unending path of suffering. Instead, by using solid principles as found in the eight-fold path, we do the inner work that enables our outer reality to transform. The ripple effect this level of attention to our own process has on others is exponential. The first act of service you can bring to everyone you are going to meet is to deal with your own neuroses. Becoming self-aware and being honest to this end are the foundation of good connection.

In this heightened honesty and self-awareness, we can also more accurately ascertain whether or not to invest in a particular connection. It is important to know where our expectations and desires end, and another's agency begins. Staying clear includes accepting we all have choice and the freedom to change our minds. Do you both want the connection to continue and thrive? Do you both choose this level of consciousness in the relationship? Are you both willing and able to operate at this level? Are you both willing and able to communicate in ways that support your mutual positive expansion? This includes being able to provide a space where the other feels respected and listened to. In some scenarios, one party is not ready, willing or able to do the things that will make conscious relating a viable option. However, when both parties agree this is the path for them, how can they best proceed?

HOW DO I ADAPT MY COMMUNICATION STYLES TO FIT SOMEONE ELSE'S ATTACHMENT STYLE AND REMAIN IN MY INTEGRITY?

The first step is always awareness.

When we become truly aware of our own predicaments it is so much easier to see the same thing in others. Much pain is caused when individuals insist that their own happiness is someone else's responsibility. To truly understand our own issues and the power of being seen, heard, felt and acknowledged in all our human and glorious mess - it is essential to re-learn how to self-soothe. Can you be present with yourself? Can you be with yourself in the darkest moments, knowing it will pass, knowing that the deeper into the dark you go, the more potential for experiencing lightness and highs you will have? Using the practice of yoga provides immense steadying power for traversing the contrast of living, for learning how to get back up when we fall down. When you begin to truly know your shadow along with your immense capability for love and creativity, the seeds of intention for harmony and connection will truly take root and you will be on a surer footing for undertaking step 2.

The second step is intention.

When we are aware of what is, we also become aware of what might be. Intending for the best possible outcome for everyone involved is a good place to start. Holding a pure intention helps smooth our efforts however clumsy the attempts we make at adaptation are. Intention also guides action in line with our integrity – it is a focus on the quality and essence rather than the content alone.

The third step is meta-communication (and honesty).

Or how we communicate about how we're communicating. An example of this could be that you recognize you got triggered because of something that was said to you by a person you spend a lot of time with. You realize this type of interaction has happened more than once. You have awareness of what happened, you have intention for a better result, for more harmony and less disruption and now you communicate these two important things to the other person with a view to improving things between you.

Unlike the first two steps which can take place in isolation, this step may feel the most challenging as it involves being vulnerably honest with someone else and asking for what you want. In vulnerable sharing there is always the possibility of re-experiencing shame. In asking there is always the possibility of being refused. Therefore, at this point many people prefer to close down or retreat from relating altogether rather than feel vulnerable. It is simply too confronting. Interestingly, we tend to unconsciously choose people to get close with who will present us with our unsolved childhood issues. Running from the person delivering the message does not change the message.

Practical points for handling this encounter bravely and well with a fighting chance of a successful outcome are as follows:

a) **Get fully resourced first – rested, fed, centered**
b) **Assuming you already have clear awareness of what happened for you, set your intention**
c) **Agree a time and place for the conversation that suits both (i.e. they can also be fully resourced)**
d) **Own your response, use responsible language (E.g. Instead of 'You made me feel' use 'I felt')**
e) **Listen well. Commit to staying present in the moment**

If you're tired, hungry, still angry or upset or determined to be right at all costs – chances are the repair attempt will almost certainly fail.

Noticing your responses and taking care of them and taking space for yourself, is a massive part of conscious connection.

Becoming responsible for our own wellbeing lets others off the hook.

To keep creating evidence that you can enable your own happiness creates a wonderful cushion of confidence from which to enter any kind of relating. From here two good things happen. Firstly, we begin to prioritize treating ourselves well, in ways that promote satisfaction and expansion. In the doing of this, we become full, vibrant and creative – able to contribute and share our natural gifts easily.

Secondly, when we realize how good it feels to take care of ourselves on all levels, it is easier to identify and learn from situations that do not support our thriving, rather than become disheartened and overpowered by them.

There is no attainment only a spiral of experience.

Revisiting, relearning and new realizations are all part of the yogic path. The return to the true self is a back and forth journey while we are in human form – a strange trick of the light that contains both forgetting and remembering.

CHAPTER 7
INNER PEACE

A ll of this is to say that it is hard to be a human sometimes and that acknowledging the challenges we face goes some way to developing useful and wholesome processes that create wellbeing and peace. Allegiance to Gods and Leaders – compelling as it may be to be led - is no substitute for doing the inner work of acknowledging your own sovereignty.

Transience remains a ghostly shadow in my psyche, the ever-present hint of death at my shoulder as Carlos Castaneda put it. I think it's the only way to truly live and I view it now as a necessary reminder to remain present, to communicate to the absolute best of my ability and to love every moment for its own sake whether its purpose be learning and evolution or pure pleasure of being here.

To remain in optimistic curiosity about living rather than nihilistic depression is always my intention, despite the often-overwhelming knowledge of my relative insignificance in an unfathomably expansive universe. I have found no better way of doing this than through the experiences brought to me through daily practices of mind and body and a commitment to refining the aspects of myself that tend to bring results I don't like. It is an ongoing process without end in sight that contains both a satisfying and deeply moving sense of accomplishment. Reviewing the quality of one's life by measuring the nature, depth and variety of the connections it contains, is perhaps the only scale we truly need.

The immeasurable wisdom contained in yoga as a system continually surprises me the more I learn about the brain and body. Western medicine is just beginning to fully ascertain the beneficial effects of this practice on emotional, social and physical health. My gratitude for this practice grows, especially every time I hit a bump in my life - it has without fail carried me over all of them. What it really comes down to is best described by a female friend of mine who, when asked why she practiced, said simply "Because my life is too painful without it."

The choice to think, do and be that which will ultimately allow us to accept the things meant for us, to flow with grace and ease, is in our hands at every moment.

Every moment and every breath are a chance to start again.

While you are still breathing you have potential, you have been given another go at living in a way that fills you up, creatively satisfies you and nourishes your soul. In the doing of this you participate in life and contribute goodness effortlessly.

Imagine what a world we'd create if living this way was a priority,

if our connection to source and ability to connect with others from this nurtured place was made important. Thriving communities start with thriving individuals who have a solid awareness of their interdependence with others and know that violence and lack for one means violence and lack for all.

Environmental, social and economic patterns, all can be positively influenced by this way of living, but it starts from the center.

It begins from our own centers, at our essence, we are each a single drop of the oceanic whole.

Love and respect for this yogic path will teach you to have love and respect for your own true nature and all the human parts of you that are still becoming.

From this place, you radiate, knowing that you are already home.

From this place you see those around you clearly, in their divinity and in their humanity.

Here   is   where   connection   thrives.

BIBLIOGRAPHY

1. The Body Keeps the Score, Mind, Brain & Body in the Transformation of Trauma – Bessel van der Kolk (2015)
2. Healing Your Attachment Wounds – Diane Poole Heller PHD (2017)
3. Loving What Is – Byron Katie (2002)
4. Perfect Love, Imperfect Relationships – John Welwood (2005)
5. Tao, The Three Treasures – Osho (1976)
6. Living Dangerously – Osho (2011)
7. Polishing the Mirror – Ram Dass (2013)

© Jemima House 2018
First edition June 2018

.

36506095R00048

Printed in Great Britain
by Amazon